Old Man Dreaming

Old Man Dreaming

A Theological Essay on Vision

John L. Williams

WIPF & STOCK • Eugene, Oregon

OLD MAN DREAMING
A Theological Essay on Vision

Copyright © 2017 John L. Williams. All rights reserved. Except for brief quotations in critical publications or reviews, no part of this book may be reproduced in any manner without prior written permission from the publisher. Write: Permissions, Wipf and Stock Publishers, 199 W. 8th Ave., Suite 3, Eugene, OR 97401.

Wipf & Stock
An Imprint of Wipf and Stock Publishers
199 W. 8th Ave., Suite 3
Eugene, OR 97401

www.wipfandstock.com

PAPERBACK ISBN: 978-1-5326-1694-5
HARDCOVER ISBN: 978-1-4982-4101-4
EBOOK ISBN: 978-1-4982-4100-7

Manufactured in the U.S.A.   JULY 18, 2017

Except where noted, Scripture quotations are from the New Revised Standard Version Bible, copyright © 1989, Division of Christian Education of the National Council of the Churches of Christ in the United States of America. Used by permission. All rights reserved.

Your old men shall dream dreams,
and your young men shall see visions.

JOEL 2:28B

Contents

Acknowledgements | *ix*
Introduction | *xi*

1. Vision and Visioning in Secular Organizations | 1
2. Vision and Visioning in Church Organizations | 10
3. The Bible's Earlier Vision Stories | 22
4. Challenging Contemporary Concepts about Vision | 35
5. Expanding Perspectives: More Texts about Vision | 56
6. Toward Understanding Vision | 74
7. A Vision for the Presbyterian Church (U.S.A.), Part 1: Seeing the Present | 105
8. A Vision for the Presbyterian Church (U.S.A.), Part 2: Visualizing Paths toward the Future | 123

Epilogue: Questions at a Threshold | *141*
Bibliography | *145*
Index | *149*

Acknowledgements

FRIENDS AND COLLEAGUES JOE Carle, Clifton Kirkpatrick, John Langfitt, and Joseph D. Small read, discussed, and offered their suggestions about my earlier ideas, papers, and book chapters. Without their challenges and our conversations from 2010 to 2016, I could not have written this book.

A friend and fellow Presbyterian, Martha Collins, shared her editorial skills, challenged me to consider my readers, and taught me to use fewer and clearer words. Because of her, I look like a better writer than I really am.

Princeton Theological Seminary reference librarian Kate Skrebutenas supported my research, opened to me the resources of a world-class theological library, and assisted me in locating specific resources.

Through the generosity of Austin Presbyterian Theological Seminary President Ted Wardlaw, I spent a day with seven of Austin Seminary's faculty: Lewis Donelson, William Greenway, Paul Hooker, David Jensen, Blair Monie, Song Park, and Cynthia Rigby. Each of them read a draft of my manuscript, and each shared her or his comments, questions, and suggestions. Thanks to these conversations, I replaced entirely one chapter and revised the other chapters.

Linda, my spouse, deserves a medal for tolerating my focus on my writing. She read everything I wrote and made helpful suggestions for improvement.

Acknowledgements

Our daughter, Kathy Wagner, who is a good writer and amateur theologian in her own right, also read some of the book's chapters and offered her comments and suggestions.

Office of the General Assembly staff Kay Moore and Terri Stephenson assisted me with some bibliographical references.

Magda Caraballo and Holly Fuller gave me good tips and valuable assistance in word processing.

Introduction

IN AN ERA WHEN interest in vision, vision statements, and visioning processes seems to have waxed, waned, and then waxed again in the Presbyterian Church (U.S.A.), why have Presbyterians and Presbyterian congregations willingly borrowed visioning processes designed for business and other secular organizations? In the Presbyterian Church, where biblical preaching has been the norm, why is so little attention paid to the Bible's stories and texts about vision(s)? And, in the Presbyterian Church that so strongly adheres to the "essential tenets" of Reformed theology, why is so little written or said about a theology of vision or vision's place in theology? These questions puzzled me for over a decade.

Then came my retirement. After more than forty years of ministry as a pastor, presbytery associate, presbytery executive, and synod executive, I had an opportunity to study and write about these questions. I assumed that I could write what I needed or wanted to say about vision in two or three papers or articles. But as I delved into the subject, I discovered more than I anticipated, more questions to ponder and more threads of thought to follow. With the encouragement and critiques of a few old friends and ministry colleagues, I continued to explore, to reflect, and to write about vision until I eventually wrote not just a few articles, but the chapters for this book.

INTRODUCTION

Based on my study, I believe there is a profound contrast between biblical and theological understandings of vision and visioning and organizational and management understandings. In organization and management theories, visions have a human origin and are given primarily to managers. Such visions are presumed to be always about the future and are limited to organizational concerns and ends. In the Bible and in theology, visions have a divine, not a human, origin; are diverse in their subjects; roam across a range of time perspectives; are given to a diversity of people; and point beyond themselves to larger purposes. Biblical and theological understandings of vision and visioning are richer, more diverse, and more profound than those found in organizational theories and management techniques.

To make my case for the richness and profundity of Christianity's understanding of vision and visioning vis-à-vis organization theories and management techniques, I summarize and critically analyze the views of those who have written on vision and visioning, first in contemporary secular organizations (chapter 1), and then in church organizations (chapter 2). I also raise important questions for leaders of both secular and church organizations to ponder.

In the next three chapters, I identify and interpret some key biblical texts about vision. I specifically differentiate the concept of vision in a group of the Bible's vision stories from concepts of vision in modern organizations. I also identify other biblical texts about vision that enrich and expand our perspectives on vision.

In chapter 6 I articulate a theology of vision and explore vision's place in theology. I define vision and describe three types of vision. Chapter 6 also includes an interlude on imagination, a discussion of christological and canonical tests for determining whether or not human visions are from God, a section on the story of the man born blind in John 9, and a concluding section on practical applications of vision and visioning in Christian communities.

In accord with my own advice at the conclusion of chapter 6 not to limit visions to a future time perspective, I present my vision for the Presbyterian Church (U.S.A.) in two parts: "Seeing the Present" (chapter 7) and "Visualizing Paths toward the Future" (chapter 8). Chapter 7 also explains the origin of the book's title.

I focus on the Presbyterian Church (U.S.A.) at the end of this book because I am a lifelong Presbyterian and because the Presbyterian Church is the only church that I know well enough to write intelligently about. I do not intend for this focus to exclude anyone—ecumenical friends and partners, interfaith friends and partners, or even secular friends—from conversations about the types of visions God has given us.

1

Vision and Visioning in Secular Organizations

According to George Barna, founder of the Barna Group, a market research firm specializing in Americans' religious beliefs and behavior, "vision became the hottest topic around"[1] in the early 1990s. Major corporations began searching for visionary leadership. Publishers and booksellers profited from business books on vision. Management professors and consultants extolled vision as the motivating energy behind organizational success; and Peter Senge, Senior Lecturer at the MIT Sloan School of Management, typified the outlook of the 1990s when he referred to a shared vision as "a force in people's hearts, a force of impressive power."[2]

But is an organization's vision always "a force of impressive power," a compelling and motivating energy driving organizational success? Contrary to Senge, there is ample anecdotal evidence that visions and visioning processes are not always powerful or successful. Sometimes visioning processes ignore or even exclude key organizational stakeholders. Sometimes visions have little or no influence over work objectives, budgets, or organizational structures. Many a vision statement resides in a file drawer, long forgotten by the organization it was supposed to guide. Such occurrences undermine visions and visioning as energizing forces.

1. Barna, *Power of Vision*, 8.
2. Senge, *Fifth Discipline*, 206.

We may eventually correct or avoid these particular human errors; but they foreshadow the results of deeper, more profound analyses of vision and visioning in secular organizations.

Two types of analyses challenge the idea that visions and visioning act as energizing forces in organizations. The first type is an analysis of the ideas and statements of those who argue for the necessity of vision and visioning in organizations. In this analysis I will pay attention to vision's definition, source(s), time perspective(s), benefits, and recipients as well as concepts related to visioning processes. The second type of analysis is an analysis of the contemporary contexts in which organizations operate and of the assumptions behind vision and visioning as they function in these contexts. A thoughtful opponent of vision's and visioning's necessity will represent this perspective.

Vision Tamed

In the 1990s certain writers in the fields of business and management asserted that an organization's vision acted as an energizing force. A detailed analysis of their views, however, reveals a different perspective, namely, that vision frequently becomes the servant of organizational self-interests. Theoretically, a vision should guide and propel the entire organization in a particular direction; but in fact, organizational structures and leaders often co-opt and domesticate the vision for their own ends. In so doing, they limit and weaken its motivating power.

Peter Senge clearly asserted vision's motivating power. His primary interest was in building "learning organizations, organizations where people continually expand their capacity to create the results they truly desire."[3] Senge argued that an ensemble of five integrated disciplines—personal mastery, mental models, building shared vision, team learning, and systems thinking—is essential for the construction of learning organizations. Vision, which he

---

3. Ibid., 3.

defined as "a specific destination, a picture of a desired future,"[4] is an essential component of two of the five disciplines, personal mastery and building shared vision. According to Senge, vision is merely one of several organizational building blocks.

When Senge identified vision's source(s) and described the visioning process, his picture of vision's organizational servitude came into full view. For Senge vision begins with the discipline of personal mastery; it begins within an individual human being, usually a leader or manager of an organization, who clarifies and deepens her/his personal vision.[5] The discipline of shared vision then builds on individual visions and lifts them to a group, communal, or corporate level. Senge, however, did not outline a definitive process for moving personal visions to a shared vision. He urged leaders to share openly their personal visions and to see building shared vision as ongoing, never-ending, and central to their daily work. He wrote:

> Visions that are truly shared take time to emerge. They grow as a by-product of interactions of individual visions. Experience suggests that visions that are genuinely shared require ongoing conversation where individuals not only feel free to express their dreams, but learn how to listen to each other's dreams. Out of this listening new insights into what is possible gradually emerge.[6]

This is as close as Senge came to defining a visioning process. It is principally an ongoing conversation, a conversation among organizational leaders that originated with their mental pictures of their organization's future.

Senge's statements on the benefits of vision augment the picture of vision's organizational servitude. "Shared vision," Senge wrote, "is vital for the learning organization because it provides the focus and energy for learning."[7] "A shared vision . . . uplifts people's aspirations. Work becomes part of . . . a larger purpose

4. Ibid., 149.
5. Ibid., 7, 141–42.
6. Ibid., 217–18.
7. Ibid., 206.

embodied in the organization's products and services."[8] "Visions are exhilarating. They create the spark . . . that lifts an organization out of the mundane."[9] "A shared vision changes people's relationship with the company. It is no longer 'their company'; it becomes 'our company.'"[10] Note that in each of these quotations an organization or its leaders are the beneficiaries of vision. Vision is thus seen as serving organizational interests even when it excites or motivates people.

Another writer, Burt Nanus, Professor Emeritus at the University of Southern California, also affirmed vision's motivating power when he opened the first chapter of his *Visionary Leadership* with the sentence, "There is no more powerful engine driving an organization toward excellence and long-range success than an attractive, worthwhile, and achievable vision of the future, widely shared."[11] He affirmed vision's future focus and limited its scope to organizations when he defined vision as "a realistic, credible, attractive future for your organization"[12] and "a mental model of a future state of a process, a group, or an organization."[13]

Nanus' views on the origin of vision were compatible with Senge's. He asserted that vision comes from organizational leaders' values, information, foresight, insight, imagination, and judgment.[14] Unlike Senge, however, Nanus clearly outlined an extensive visioning process in steps or tasks that include describing the organization's characteristics, examining its current vision, identifying its stakeholders, imagining different organizational visions, selecting the right vision, and sharing it in the organization.[15] Accompanying these and other tasks are questions to be answered and subtasks to be performed.

8. Ibid., 207–8.
9. Ibid., 208.
10. Ibid.
11. Nanus, *Visionary Leadership*, 3.
12. Ibid., 8.
13. Ibid., 25.
14. Ibid., 34–35.
15. Ibid., chs. 3–6.

VISION AND VISIONING IN SECULAR ORGANIZATIONS

Writer John P. Kotter, Professor of Leadership Emeritus at the Harvard Business School, also sang vision's praises. He wrote: "Of the . . . elements that are always found in successful transformations, none is more important than a sensible vision."[16] At the same time, he placed vision squarely in an organizational context when he identified visioning as part of the third stage of a longer eight-stage process for creating major change in an organization. He defined vision simply as "a picture of the future,"[17] but then argued that effective visions have six organizational characteristics: an imaginable future, desirable for most organizational stakeholders, realistic and attainable, clear enough to guide decisions, flexible enough to allow initiative, and easy to communicate.[18]

Kotter's visioning process was not steps to be followed in sequence, as Nanus outlined, nor were they the absence of steps, as in Senge's thought. He described them in the form of advice based on his experience as an observer of companies trying to create visions for change. Expect the guiding coalition to guide the process, he advised. "Developing a good vision is an exercise of both the head and the heart, it takes some time, it always involves a group of people, and it is tough to do well."[19] Do not mistake the brevity of Kotter's phrases for simple and easy. He knew that visioning in organizations requires months of effort, teamwork, complexity, and even interpersonal conflict.

Kotter lauded vision's benefits. He declared, "A good vision serves three important purposes. First, [it clarifies] the general direction for change. Second, it motivates people to take action in the right direction, even if the initial steps are personally painful. Third, it helps coordinate the actions of different people . . . in a remarkably fast and effective way."[20] Each purpose serves organizational interests.

16. Kotter, *Leading Change*, 7.
17. Ibid., 68.
18. Ibid., 71–72.
19. Ibid., 79.
20. Ibid., 68–69.

Old Man Dreaming

All three writers praised vision for its motivating power and its importance; and they defined it as an image of the future. They also confined it to particular organizational contexts; and they argued that its source was people within the organization, usually the organization's leaders and managers. Their visioning processes focused on organizational interests, and they understood vision's benefits to be to the organization's advantage. In effect, they extolled vision and then quickly tamed it.

None of the three identified a vision's recipients; but because each was interested in the role and function of vision in an organization, we may infer that a vision's recipients are most likely the organization's leaders and managers. In other words, the very same people who are vision's source(s) are also its recipients. There is no essential distinction between a vision's source and its recipients, no differentiation between a vision's author and its receiver. The organizational visionary gets his/her own vision.

Vision Impossible

While writers were praising and then taming vision's power, Ralph Stacey, Professor of Management at the University of Hertfordshire in the UK, was examining the assumptions inherent in contemporary organizational contexts and in vision and visioning processes. Writing primarily for business managers, he saw the context of business organizations not simply as changing, but as turbulent. In such a context old assumptions about the marks of business success, such as "an organization should have a common and unified culture" or "Success is . . . a state of stable equilibrium,"[21] no longer work. Stacey referred to these assumptions as "traditional navigational principles" or "old maps." "An old map is useless when the terrain is new," he said. "Old beliefs cannot help in the task managers face today: managing the unknowable."[22] He argued that "in organizations the links between cause and effect can be complex,

---

21. Stacey, *Managing the Unknowable*, 2.
22. Ibid., 3–4.

distant in time and space, and very difficult to detect,"[23] and that "the future is inherently unpredictable."[24] Based on observations and analyses of contemporary organizational environments, Stacey challenged widely held beliefs about how organizations can and should operate.

Stacey singled out ideas on the role and importance of vision and intention for particular scrutiny. He reviewed studies of links between vision and plans and organizational success, and concluded, "There is . . . no reliable evidence that visions of the future and plans lead to improved performance."[25]

Stacey also examined "the role of intention in strategic management,"[26] that is, the role of vision and prior intention in an organization's strategic decisions. Of a very common understanding of vision, namely, vision as a picture of the future state or destination of an organization, Stacey concluded, "The advice to form a vision is not concrete enough to be useful, nor does it produce something possible to achieve because the future is unknowable."[27] The basic assumptions on which vision and visioning processes rest, stable equilibrium, linear thinking, predictability, and cohesion, no longer function in turbulent environments.

If the assumptions on which vision and visioning rest no longer work, can an organization ever determine its strategic direction(s)? It can, said Stacey. He argued that strategic direction(s) emerge from what managers do, not from prior intentions or visions, and that intention in organizations is best understood as intention to be creative, not intention to reach a future, unknowable destination.[28]

23. Ibid., 11.
24. Ibid., 13.
25. Ibid., 27.
26. Ibid., 126–45.
27. Ibid., 137.
28. Ibid., 146.

A Note to Church Leaders

In recent decades congregations and church organizations have borrowed and adapted for their own use visioning processes originally designed for secular organizations. Sometimes they've also employed management consultants to lead them in those processes. While there are many possible reasons for doing so, I suspect that one of the primary reasons was a search for clarity in a complex and tumultuous world. This is a search I can easily understand. In my ministry I often wished that my congregation or my judicatory had a greater or at least a modest amount of clarity, especially clarity of direction or clarity of purpose.

My reflections on vision and visioning processes raise some questions. Do we want a vision that only pretends to be a driving force in an organization, a vision easily co-opted by organizational or institutional self-interests? Do we want a visioning process that presupposes an equilibrium and a cohesion that no longer exists? Our congregations and church organizations obviously live in the same turbulence that surrounds all other organizations.

When we borrow someone else's management technique, such as a visioning process, we get the technique's weaknesses and assumptions along with its strengths. When we hire a consultant, we get the consultant's presuppositions. But do we know what a management technique assumes or a consultant presupposes about vision and visioning? Have we even asked? And, have we considered whether or not these assumptions are consistent with our beliefs and values, our theology and ethics, consistent with the witness of the Bible and the witness of our creeds and confessions?

A friend of mine was once asked to serve as an advisor to a group whose chief responsibility was visioning and planning in a congregation. Twice my friend recommended that the group study some biblical resources on vision, and twice the group said that they were not interested. Apparently the group wanted to complete their work as soon as possible. They accepted a visioning process familiar to them from secular organizations, with all its unexamined assumptions, rather than enter the unfamiliar territory of the

Bible's stories and words about vision. My friend's experience illustrates our dilemma with respect to vision and visioning. We are caught between the familiar, but weakened and presupposition-laden, visions of secular organizations and the unfamiliar, but challenging and promising, visions of biblical faith.

In these circumstances we owe it to ourselves to think twice before we borrow management techniques or employ management consultants, but not because we believe such techniques or consultants are wrong, weak, valueless, or baseless. Management techniques and consultants do have some utility. We owe it to ourselves to think twice because we affirm that our real source of clarity, our real source of vision, is not in processes developed for secular organizations, but in the triune God, the creator, redeemer, and sustainer of all.

2

Vision and Visioning in Church Organizations

IDEAS ON VISION IN church organizations differ somewhat from ideas on vision in secular organizations. But are they sufficiently different to release vision from organizational self-interests? Does vision become a compelling and motivating energy, a force challenging a congregation or religious organization to new or revitalized ministry and mission? Or, will organizational structures and leaders co-opt it for their own ends? And, what are their assumptions about vision and visioning processes?

Barna and Mancini

Both George Barna and Will Mancini, founder of Auxano, a church vision consulting group, advocated the use of vision and visioning processes in churches; and Barna agreed with secular writers in praise of vision. His praise was extravagant. "Because the vision becomes the driving force in your sense of purpose, it reshapes your personality and your behavior to a significant degree,"[1] he wrote. "Vision, then, becomes a bold reason for living."[2]

---

1. Barna, *Power of Vision*, 86.
2. Ibid., 88.

Vision and Visioning in Church Organizations

Barna's definition of vision both resembled and differed from secular definitions. "Vision for ministry is a clear mental image of a preferable future imparted by God to His chosen servants and is based upon an accurate understanding of God, self and circumstances,"[3] he said. Although his definition of vision as "a clear mental image of a preferable future" was similar to secular definitions, he narrowed his definition to "vision for ministry." From the outset he confined vision to work ordinarily carried out within a congregational organization.

Barna clearly disagreed with secular writers about vision's source. Vision comes from God alone, not from any human source. Authors who "underscore the importance of vision in the business world . . . fail to include an irreplaceable factor in the equation from a Christian perspective: the mind of God."[4]

Barna identified a vision's recipients precisely in his definition with the phrase "imparted by God to His chosen servants." Who are the "chosen servants"? Barna identified them as pastors of congregations when he wrote, "Visionary leaders receive their vision for ministry from God."[5] "The future belongs to visionary pastors."[6] He also designed a visioning process exclusively for pastors.[7] Only pastors, according to Barna, receive visions for ministry.

We may outline Barna's views as follows: God gives compelling visions for ministry to pastors who share those visions with their congregations. We might call this a hierarchy of vision, with God above, pastors in the middle, and people below. Such a hierarchy raises theological questions.

(1) Does not this type of hierarchy conflict with the priesthood of all believers, an evangelical article of faith? The sixteenth-century Reformers intentionally asserted the priesthood of all believers to remove the unscriptural distinctions, the class differentials, between clergy and laity, and to give the laity equal access

---

3. Ibid., 24.
4. Ibid., 59–60.
5. Ibid., 26.
6. Ibid., 29.
7. Ibid., ch. 6.

to the Bible and the sacraments. Does Barna's hierarchy of vision, perhaps inadvertently, introduce a new distinction between pastor and people? It would seem so. Barna apparently believes that God gives visions for ministry only to pastors directly and to laity indirectly through a pastoral intermediary.

(2) Who is the real mediator between God and the people? The letter to the Hebrews speaks of Jesus Christ as "the mediator of the new covenant."[8] First Timothy 2:5–6 says, "For there is one God; there is also one mediator between God and humankind, Christ Jesus, himself human, who gave himself a ransom for all." Pastors are indeed ambassadors for Christ, but they are not the mediators between God and humankind. Yet Barna's hierarchy of vision seems to put them in that position.

(3) How does Barna's vision hierarchy account for human sin? Barna claims that God's visions for ministry are perfect, blessed, and inspired.[9] That may be true, but the recipients of such visions are definitely not perfect and are not always blessed or inspired.

Barna's visioning process was extensive and complex. He titled his chapter on discerning vision "Capturing God's Vision"; and he wrote to pastors, "You must be prepared to invest yourself in the acquisition process."[10] He then summarized his acquisition process as follows: "First, you must know yourself. Second, you must know the ministry environment in which you reside. Third, you must know God intimately. Fourth, you must gain objective wisdom related to your search."[11] Each of the four steps included long lists of questions or tasks for a pastor to answer or perform. Step one appeared to be a ministerial version of career or psychological self-assessment processes and seemed somewhat similar to Senge's discipline of personal mastery. Step two was a sociological assessment of a congregation's surrounding community.

Barna's description of vision's benefits was in effect a picture of vision's organizational servitude. Barna declared that there are

---

8. Heb 8:6; 9:15; 12:24.
9. Barna, *Power of Vision*, 64.
10. Ibid., 70.
11. Ibid., 70–71.

nine characteristics of God's vision for pastoral ministry: inspiring, change oriented, challenging, empowering, long-term, customized, detailed, people oriented, and a revelation of a promising future.[12] Pastors ordinarily experience these benefits or characteristics in a particular organizational setting, namely, a congregation.

Will Mancini, in contrast with secular writers and with Barna, defined vision in a somewhat novel fashion when he called vision proper "the living language that anticipates and illustrates God's better intermediate future."[13] He distinguished between the ultimate, final, eschatological future, which is in God's hands alone, and an intermediate future between now and God's final end times, in which humankind may join with God in mission.

Mancini agreed with Barna against our secular writers: vision comes from God alone. He added, "As each leader relates, rules, and rescues with God in this messy world, God reveals to him or her a better intermediate future to pursue. That is, God speaks in their hearts new ideas, new aspirations, and new mental pictures of what could be."[14]

Although Barna and Mancini agreed on vision's source, they differed on vision's recipients. Mancini never identified precisely a vision's recipients, although he did use the terms "missional leaders" or simply "leaders" throughout his book. We may infer from his use of such terms that he understood a vision's recipients to be a congregation's or religious organization's missional leaders, either laity or clergy.

Mancini's visioning process was as extensive as Barna's; and, as we might expect from the difference in recipients, his process steps are more clearly related to a congregation's work and mission than to an individual's ministry. Mancini divided visioning into two major stages: clarifying vision and articulating vision. "The starting point for vision—for thinking about our church's future—is not deciding where we want to go or exploring what is working for other churches

---

12. Ibid., 86–93.
13. Mancini, *Church Unique*, 170.
14. Ibid., 72.

but understanding how we are unique,"[15] he wrote. To help a congregation understand its uniqueness, he posed to a congregation's leadership questions about their community's unique needs and opportunities, their congregation's unique resources and capabilities, their leadership's interests and passions, and what they can do better than other congregations.[16] Stage 1, clarifying vision, is actually an exercise in organizational assessment.

In moving from clarifying vision to articulating vision, Mancini observed that understanding a congregation's uniqueness is "not the words you use to cast vision."[17] To cast vision, he introduced his vision frame, which he described as "five components that define your church's DNA and create the platform for all vision casting."[18] Think of the first four components as the four sides of a rectangular picture frame and the fifth component as the picture in the frame that Mancini called "vision proper."[19] Mancini identified two of the first four components as strategy and measures of accomplishment. Vision proper, therefore, is a particular congregation's vision and is framed on two of its sides by strategy and measures, by organizational concerns.

Mancini specifically listed the benefits of the strategy side of the vision frame. Strategy, said Mancini, "shows how to accomplish the mission with a few right ministries, . . . clarifies a simple pathway of involvement, . . . limits and stewards time 'at church' to release people to 'be church,' . . . filters which ideas fit best and which ones don't, [and] guides people through a balanced process of discipleship."[20] Without exception these are benefits to a congregation as an organization.

Mancini titled the final section of his book "Advancing Vision" and included chapters on structural alignment and creating attunement. "The vision will not move forward unless it ties into

15. Ibid., 6.
16. Ibid., 84–85, 98.
17. Ibid., 111.
18. Ibid., 113.
19. Ibid.
20. Ibid., 150.

and brings together leadership, communication, processes, environments, and culture. If it does, your church unique will capture your culture and build a movement that flows into your community with contagious redemptive passion."[21] In other words, vision works best in an organization when everything else aligns with it. But what if leadership, communication, and other factors do not align with vision? Mancini's own words are an implicit acknowledgment that church leadership and structures can and sometimes do fail to align with a congregation's or a church organization's vision.

But are Barna's and Mancini's ideas about vision sufficiently different from secular ideas to release vision from organizational self-interest? Does vision become a compelling and motivating force challenging a congregation to new or revitalized ministry or mission? Not necessarily. Will organizational leaders and structures co-opt vision for their own ends, even though the organization is a congregation or another church organization? Yes, and evidence supports this contention. Barna's limitation of vision to pastors and their ministry, his references to vision discernment as a "capturing" or an "acquisition process," and his list of vision's organizational benefits suggest organizational self-interest. Mancini's clarifying vision as an exercise in identifying a congregation's uniqueness, his description of vision proper as the vision of a particular congregation framed by organizational concerns, his list of organizational benefits, and his tacit admission that structures and leaders do not always align with vision—these too suggest organizational self-interest.

It is noteworthy that neither Barna nor Mancini identified or examined any assumptions about vision or visioning processes, much less whether or not such assumptions might be feasible.

Other Perspectives

Based on her extensive experience in international relief, economic and social development, and a church agency, Sandra Swan

21. Ibid., 233.

wrote a manual for anyone who wants to start a new philanthropic, charitable, or outreach program or to transform an old program. She assumed that her readers desire to be both compassionate and competent and that they seek effective, cost-efficient, and long-lasting solutions to an economic or social problem's root causes.[22] She subtitled her manual "Doing Good the Better Way."

According to Swan, this better way distinguishes clearly among three key development terms: resource or input, activity or output, and result or impact/outcome/goal.[23] The better way also begins the process of developing or transforming philanthropic programs not by working on resources or activities, but by determining the desired results. "Our first step . . . is to focus on what problem we want to solve, and what the solution would look like if we accomplish it,"[24] Swan said. This step involves researching a particular problem and its solution(s), consulting with members of affected communities, and identifying root causes as opposed to symptoms.

Once the result, impact, outcome, or goal of a charitable or outreach program is identified, the development process shifts "to focus on the activities that would solve the problem,"[25] said Swan. "Activities (*outputs*) are intermediate steps that use resources (*inputs*) to lead us to the solution, the desired result (the *impact*)."[26] Advocacy is an example of an activity that might be necessary in order to change attitudes, cultures, systems, or laws.[27] Once the necessary activities are identified, the development process shifts once again, this time to resources, to "any asset, or attribute, or quality, or supply that can be gathered and channeled so it can be employed in a philanthropic program."[28] Potential partners

---

22. Swan, *New Outreach*, ix–xi, 2–5.
23. Ibid., 19, 83.
24. Ibid., 7.
25. Ibid., 9.
26. Ibid., 35.
27. Ibid., 12–13.
28. Ibid., 20.

and members of affected communities are examples of human resources that might be employed in such a program.

Swan's views on resources merit elaboration. She observed that resources are either tangible, such as money, equipment, building space, or tools, or intangible, such as talent, abilities, skills, expertise, knowledge, experience, enthusiasm, passion, or personal contacts.[29] Then she noted "the three resources that are more important than all others combined when it comes to solving problems: vision, creativity, and imagination."[30] She called them "The Big Three," and she defined vision as "the ability to conjure up a picture of the world as we want it to be."[31] Note that these three resources may be employed in all three phases of the development or transformative process. But more important, note the striking difference between Swan's concept of vision and Barna's, Mancini's, and most secular writers' concepts of vision. For Swan, vision is not an organizational or institutional goal or purpose to be achieved. It is not a final destination toward which an organization or institution is or should be moving. For Swan, vision, creativity, and imagination are talents and abilities within individuals, talents and abilities that they may share and use in development or transformative processes. Although she did not cite 1 Corinthians 12, Swan seemed to believe that vision, creativity, and imagination are among Paul's "varieties of gifts."[32]

My two published articles related to vision are another, albeit incomplete, perspective on vision in church organizations. In my first article I wanted to view the Presbyterian Church (U.S.A.) as a whole, to look at my denomination through the widest possible lens.[33] I made two observations: (1) God has blessed the Presbyterian Church with a variety of gifts; (2) God is confronting the Presbyterian Church with critical challenges. I envisioned a church

---

29. Ibid., 19–20.
30. Ibid., 27.
31. Ibid.
32. 1 Cor 12:4–11.
33. Williams, "Envisioning the Presbyterian Church (U.S.A.)."

that receives and cultivates God's gifts and hears and confronts the challenges before it.

In hindsight, I have two impressions of my first article. (1) My ideas on vision were definitely incomplete. I did not define vision, although one could reasonably infer that I understood vision to be a mental image. I did not specifically identify my vision's source(s), its time perspective(s), or its recipients. I did not describe a visioning process. (2) I managed to cast a vision with relatively fewer organizational constraints than those found in the writings of others. For example, I did not confine vision's source to particular organizational leaders. I did not limit vision to a particular congregation, ministry, or religious organization, although I did envision a denominational future, a context with organizational perimeters. And, I did not promise organizational benefits.

My second article was a reply to another person's paper and related to vision in only two respects.[34] First, I stated my belief that organizational fixes will not solve the Presbyterian Church's more deeply rooted dilemmas. Second, I identified a few foundational and systemic work areas that might be used to effectively propel the Presbyterian Church into a healthier long-term future. Although I did not call these work areas "vision," I in effect cast vision not as an image of a final state or an end product, but as a pathway or pathways by which we might join in God's ongoing mission.

Like Barna and Mancini, neither Swan nor I identified or examined our assumptions about vision, visioning processes, or the feasibility of our assumptions.

Comments and Questions

Except for the fact that church organizations claim that God is the source of vision, church organizations and secular organizations are far more alike than different with respect to vision and visioning processes. Both types of organizations define vision in much the same way (Swan's definition is an exception). Both assert

---

34. Williams, "Thought Provoking," 54–59.

that vision is about the future. Both create visioning processes that are substantively alike, although they differ in detail. Both praise vision's motivating power, while in both it succumbs to organizational or institutional self-interest. Both make assumptions, usually unexamined, about the nature of the environments in which their organizations function and about the ability of human beings to predict the future. Because secular and church organizations share similar perspectives on vision and visioning, it is appropriate to offer a critique and raise questions about both together.

Whether from secular or church organizations, all of our writers stated or at least implied that vision is some type of mental image of a state to be achieved or a destination to be reached; and all wrote as if such a definition is self-evident. But is it really self-evident that vision is a mental image of a future state or destination? Are there other forms and other definitions of vision? We need to reflect deeply and analytically on the nature and definition(s) of vision and to reconsider our assumptions about vision and visioning processes. Such reconsideration might prevent exaggerated claims. I will explore the nature of vision in chapter 6.

In a similar fashion, we should reconsider vision's time perspective. All of our writers stated or assumed that vision is about something in the future, a future state or future set of circumstances. But are vision and visioning always about the future? Must we always articulate vision in the future tense? Serious reflection on vision's and visioning processes' relationship to time is needed. I will explore the vision-time relationship in chapter 4.

Some questions arise not from what our writers said or seemed to assume, but from their silence. For example, how does a vision's serving organizational self-interest affect a corporation's hourly, clerical, or lower managerial employees? How does it affect a church's members? What generally are the effects of vision and its organizational servitude on those who are "the least" in an organization?[35] These questions are variant forms of the question: Who are an organization's stakeholders? Are not a company's

---

35. Matt 25:40–45.

hourly employees and a congregation's members also stakeholders in addition to corporate and religious leaders?

Of the writers mentioned, only Sandra Swan considered the effects of vision and program upon "the least." She not only recommended consultation with members of affected communities when identifying a program's outcome, result(s), or goal; she also strongly recommended that the process for developing a philanthropic program be a participatory community process and that "representatives of any group that may be affected" be invited into that process "right from the start."[36] She challenged head-on common assumptions that "we" know best and that "the least" have no resources, talents, or viewpoints to share.

One topic about which all of our writers were silent was the philosophical or theological basis or foundation of each organization. What philosophical or theological ideas or concepts are behind each organization? And to what degree do those ideas or concepts determine a vision for that organization? Do they predetermine that a vision will serve organizational self-interest or overlook environmental turbulence? Of our secular writers I would ask specifically: What economic, social, or political theory forms the basis or foundation of today's organizations and institutions? To what degree do modern capitalism, social justice, or expressive individualism determine our visions? None of our secular writers delve into such questions, but I suspect that answering these questions is one of the keys to understanding why structures and leaders co-opt and domesticate vision for their own ends.

Of Barna and Mancini I would ask the same general questions, but I would revise the specific questions to read: What ecclesiology forms the basis or foundation of the congregations and religious organizations that you seek to serve? To what degree does congregational polity determine a congregation's vision, and does it predetermine a vision's serving organizational self-interest? When Barna and Mancini speak of "church," they almost always mean a particular congregation. One will search their books in vain for the Nicene marks of the church or, surprisingly, New Testament images

---

36. Swan, *New Outreach*, 82.

of the church. Surely the ecclesiology of a congregation, minister, or church consultant influences vision and visioning processes.

We should note at this point that questions about ecclesiology are not solely theoretical. They also pertain to the daily lives and practices of all congregations and church organizations, lives and practices that in my experience are rich and varied. They pertain, for example, to a congregation's liturgical practices in worship, prayer, sacrament, and song; to its web of relationships among people and pastors; to its variety of formal and informal education; and to its participation in God's mission around the block and around the world. Congregations and church organizations cannot be reduced to their administrative processes such as visioning. If anything, they require the theological underpinnings of a thoughtful ecclesiology.

Of those who wrote on vision and visioning in church organizations, I would ask one more question: Why did you not pay attention to the Bible's vision stories? Let me be clear. *The Bible does speak about vision!* I did not expect the secular writers to refer to the Bible, but the absence of attention to the Bible's vision stories by those from church organizations puzzled me. These stories are the Bible's accounts of vision's origin, subjects, time perspective(s), recipients, and purpose(s). They are the primary resource for understanding the importance, power, place, and limits of vision in Christianity. They are, in fact, indispensable to thinking about vision and visioning processes in the body of Christ and all its manifestations.

The Bible's understanding of vision, as expressed in its vision stories and other passages, differs qualitatively from contemporary understandings of vision and visioning processes, including those in church organizations. The next three chapters will focus on the Bible's understanding of vision.

3

The Bible's Earlier Vision Stories

THE MORE ONE STUDIES the Bible, the deeper one plunges into its depths, the more one encounters a vast variety of ways God and the world's people have communicated with one another. Among this variety are a small group of biblical texts that involve vision. Sometimes these texts tell stories in which God caused specific people to see something. The stories typically describe a vision and its effects. They appear in both the Hebrew Scriptures and the New Testament. Some are well known and familiar to us, while others go unnoticed. They range in length from a few sentences to several chapters. Without attempting to create or challenge any particular literary genre, I will simply call these texts vision stories.

Some Old Testament vision stories are earlier in that they are accounts of events that both happened before and were written down before Israel's postexilic era in which Jewish apocalypticism emerged. Some New Testament vision stories are earlier in that they recall events that both took place and were recorded prior to the last book in the New Testament canon, the Apocalypse of John. The Bible's earlier vision stories, whether in the Old Testament or the New, are very different from the apocalyptic visions found in some of the latter prophets, Daniel, and Revelation, although one such story does include some apocalyptic elements.

No two of the Bible's vision stories are exactly alike, not even those that repeat the same story two or three times. There is, however, enough similarity among them that they merit consideration as a group, in addition to examination of each text individually.

These stories were written long before contemporary organizations and institutions, both secular and ecclesiastical, contemplated the role of vision and adopted visioning processes as part of their work. Nevertheless, these stories, taken collectively, and sometimes individually, bear witness to an understanding of vision that is very different from contemporary understandings. These ancient texts challenge much that we believe and think we know about vision in today's organizations and society as a whole.

This chapter will focus on the characteristics of the Bible's earlier vision stories, on features that distinguish them from other stories and types of literature. Each of these stories has at least two of three characteristics. (1) A vocabulary of seeing either introduces the vision or is integral to the vision story. (2) The vision itself, what one sees, is a specific, distinct, and identifiable object, scene, event, or person. (3) The vision is transmitted from its source, God, directly to its recipient(s). There are no intermediaries between God and the recipients.

I will examine each characteristic.

Vocabulary of Seeing

In telling stories about visions, both the Hebrew Scriptures and the Greek New Testament use a vocabulary of seeing, words that basically refer to sensory perception (as in "see with one's eyes"), but may also refer to mental perception. This vocabulary is evident in the New Revised Standard Version (NRSV) and other English translations of the Bible. In order to identify this vocabulary for readers, I will in upcoming paragraphs italicize words that the NRSV translates from the Hebrew or Greek vocabulary of seeing.[1]

---

1. The vocabulary of seeing in the Hebrew Scriptures consists of two Hebrew verbs that mean "see," *ra'ah* and *chazah*, together with the nouns derived from each of them. The vocabulary of seeing in the Greek New Testament consists of four Greek verbs that mean "see, look, perceive, behold": (1) the irregular verb *horao* with its two additional roots, *optomai* and *ido* or *eido*; (2)

OLD MAN DREAMING

Most of the Old Testament's earlier vision stories introduce readers to a particular vision using one of two patterns. In the first pattern the writer begins in either the first person or the third person depending on whether or not he or she is speaking autobiographically. Next the writer uses a form of the verb "see" in either the present or past tense, concluding with a description of what one sees, the vision itself. We may diagram this pattern as follows:

> I, he, or she | appropriate tense of "see" | the vision.

Examples from the NRSV illustrate this pattern in vision stories. "Then Micaiah said, '*I saw* all Israel scattered on the mountains, like sheep that have no shepherd.'"[2] "[T]he Lord opened the eyes of the servant, and *he saw*; the mountain was full of horses and chariots of fire all around Elisha."[3] "*I saw* the Lord standing beside the alter."[4] "In the year that King Uzziah died, *I saw* the Lord."[5] "'Jeremiah, what *do you see*?' And I said, '*I see* a branch of an almond tree.'"[6] "[A]s I was among the exiles by the river Chebar, the heavens were opened, and *I saw visions* of God."[7] The italicized phrases are translations of the Hebrew vocabulary of seeing.

The second pattern changes the meaning of the verb "see" to "cause to see" or "show." It also rearranges the sentence structure so that God or the Lord becomes the subject of the sentence. We may diagram the second pattern as follows:

> God or the Lord | appropriate tense of "show" | to me, her, or him | the vision.

---

theoreo; (3) *theaomai*; and (4) *blepo*. It also includes a Greek verb that means "show," *deiknumi*, and the nouns derived primarily from *horao* and its additional roots.

2. 1 Kgs 22:17.
3. 2 Kgs 6:17.
4. Amos 9:1.
5. Isa 6:1.
6. Jer 1:11.
7. Ezek 1:1.

The Bible's Earlier Vision Stories

Examples from the NRSV illustrate this second pattern. "This is what the Lord *showed* me: he was forming locusts at the time the latter growth began to sprout."[8] Amos repeats this pattern three more times, in 7:4, 7; and 8:1, each time followed by a different vision. Jeremiah also uses this pattern in 24:1, "The Lord *showed* me two baskets of figs"; and Jeremiah 38:21–22 repeats it with a different vision. Again the italicized phrases are translations of the Hebrew vocabulary of seeing.

The story of Moses at the burning bush does not conform to either of the two patterns, but it does introduce the vision with a vocabulary of seeing. In fact, it uses three different forms of "see": a passive form that means "be seen" or "appear," two active forms, and a noun form. Note the various forms in italics in the NRSV translation:

> There the angel of the Lord *appeared* to him in a flame of fire out of a bush; he *looked* and the bush was blazing, yet it was not consumed. Then Moses said, "I must turn aside and *look* at this great *sight*."[9]

The repetition in vocabulary emphasizes vision.

One earlier vision story, the account of Abram's vision of the night sky and God's promise to give Abram descendants, uses the noun "vision" to introduce not only the vision itself, but also the entire narrative: "After these things the word of the Lord came to Abram in a *vision*."[10] The presence of the vocabulary of seeing alerts us to the vision to come. Another Old Testament vision story, the vision of the valley of dry bones,[11] does not use a vocabulary of seeing; but it does have the other characteristics of vision stories.

The New Testament's earlier vision stories also use a vocabulary of seeing; however, formulaic patterns of use are not very common. The three Synoptic accounts of the vision at Jesus' baptism, as translated in the NRSV, illustrate a diverse vocabulary of seeing

---

8. Amos 7:1.
9. Exod 3:2–3.
10. Gen 15:1.
11. Ezek 37:1–14.

in the same narrative. Mark's Gospel says of Jesus immediately following his baptism, "*[H]e saw* the heavens torn apart and the Spirit descending like a dove on him."[12] Matthew's Gospel says, "[T]he heavens were opened to him and *he saw* the Spirit of God descending like a dove."[13] Luke says, "[T]he heaven was opened, and the Holy Spirit descended upon him in bodily *form* like a dove."[14] The italicized words show the presence of the vocabulary of seeing in all three accounts, but only two of them use the same verb to introduce the vision. The third describes the vision with a noun.

The Synoptic accounts of Jesus' transfiguration display similar complexity. In all three accounts there are two visions: the first of the dazzling white, transfigured Jesus and the second of Moses and Elijah in conversation with Jesus. Of the three only Luke introduced the first vision with a vocabulary of seeing. He wrote of Jesus, "[T]he *appearance* of his face changed, and his clothes became dazzling white."[15] In contrast, all three Gospel writers described the second vision with a vocabulary of seeing. Said Mark," [T]here *appeared* to them Elijah and Moses."[16] Said Matthew, "[T]here *appeared* to them Moses and Elijah talking with him."[17] Luke wrote of "two men, Moses and Elijah, talking to him. They *appeared* in glory."[18] Then, as if the vocabulary of seeing was insufficient, Matthew wrote immediately following his account of Jesus' transfiguration, "As they were coming down the mountain, Jesus ordered them, 'Tell no one about the *vision*.'"[19]

Of the vision stories in Acts, the account of Stephen's vision after his address to the Jewish council and before his stoning clearly introduces the vision with a vocabulary of seeing. "[H]e gazed into heaven and *saw* the glory of God and Jesus standing at the right

12. Mark 1:10.
13. Matt 3:16.
14. Luke 3:21–22.
15. Luke 9:29.
16. Mark 9:4.
17. Matt 17:3.
18. Luke 9:31–31.
19. Matt 17:9.

hand of God. 'Look,' he said, '*I see* the heavens opened and the Son of Man standing at the right hand of God!'"[20]

In two of the three accounts of Saul's conversion and call, Acts 9:1–19a and 22:6–16, the vocabulary of seeing is present, but it does not introduce Saul's/Paul's vision. Instead it refers to what Saul's traveling companions did or did not see, to his temporary blindness, or to what Ananias did or did not see. But in the Acts 26 account, Paul introduces his vision to King Agrippa with the vocabulary of seeing, "I *saw* a light from heaven, brighter than the sun, shining around me and my companions."[21] A few sentences later Paul reports Jesus saying to him, "I *have appeared* to you for this purpose, to appoint you to serve and testify to the things that you *have seen* and to those in which I *will appear* to you."[22]

The two accounts of Peter's vision amid his encounter with Cornelius and his report to the church at Jerusalem feel like a return to the Old Testament's first pattern of vision introduction. Says Acts 10:11, "*He saw* the heaven opened and something like a large sheet coming down." In his report in Jerusalem, Peter opened his response to his critics, "I was in the city of Joppa praying, and in a trance *I saw a vision*."[23]

The story of Paul's vision of the man of Macedonia also uses vocabulary in a way resembling the Old Testament's first pattern. The Greek text of Acts 16:9 introduces the vision with the words, "During the night *a vision appeared* to Paul"; and it follows the vision with the words, "When *he had seen the vision*."[24] The vocabulary of seeing surrounds the pleading man of Macedonia.

We should note at this point that God has not communicated and does not communicate with people exclusively through visions. God communicated through dreams; and there are dream stories in the Bible (e.g., the Joseph stories in Genesis). A vocabulary of dreaming accompanies these stories. God has also communicated

20. Acts 7:55–56.
21. Acts 26:13.
22. Acts 26:16.
23. Acts 11:5.
24. Acts 16:10.

by speaking directly to and with people, by audition. (I am using a general definition of "audition," meaning any act of hearing, as opposed to its narrower definition, meaning a trial performance.) Auditions with their extensive vocabulary of speaking and hearing are by far the most widespread mode of divine communication in the Bible. Within the Bible, therefore, vision stories and their vocabulary do not have priority over other stories and vocabularies. Instead they stand alongside of and are in conversation with the others. They complement, not displace, the others.

Other modes of divine communication besides the earlier vision stories also use a vocabulary of seeing. Apocalyptic vision narratives use it; and angelophanies, appearances of messengers or angels who carry communication between God and recipient(s), also use it. Earlier vision stories do not have exclusive use of this vocabulary. There are even examples of auditions using a vocabulary of seeing. The presence of a vocabulary of seeing does not by itself guarantee that a story is an earlier vision story. Other characteristics must be considered.

Specific, Distinct, and Identifiable

Earlier visions, what one actually sees, are specific, distinct, and identifiable objects, scenes, events, or people. A vision's recipient does in fact see something or someone, and the recipient can in fact describe or identify who or what she or he has seen. The visions seen in these stories are relatively simple, relatively precise, and relatively easy for both the vision's recipients and the stories' readers to understand. Complexity and obscurity are not ordinarily characteristics of these visions.

The biblical accounts of the visions themselves are the best illustrations of their precision, distinctiveness, and recognizability. God showed Abram the night sky and told him to "count the stars, if you are able to count them."[25] Moses saw a bush that was ablaze,

---

25. Gen 15:5.

The Bible's Earlier Vision Stories

but not consumed.[26] Micaiah ben Imlah saw two visions: "all Israel scattered on the mountains, like sheep that have no shepherd," and "the Lord sitting on his throne, with all the host of heaven standing beside him."[27]

The Lord showed Amos five visions: the Lord "forming locusts at the time the latter growth began to sprout"[28]; the Lord "calling for a judgment by fire," which "devoured the great deep and was eating the land"[29]; "the Lord . . . standing beside a wall built with a plumb line, with a plumb line in his hand"[30]; "a basket of summer fruit"[31]; and "the Lord standing beside the alter."[32] Note how brief and precise these visions are. Note also that all five are about judgment.

The vision of Isaiah in the temple is somewhat longer than Amos' visions. In addition to "the Lord sitting on a throne, high and lofty,"[33] he also saw the Lord's robe filling the temple; the six-winged seraphs in attendance; the antiphonal "Holy, holy, holy"; the shaking of the threshold at the calling voices; and "the house filled with smoke."[34] Isaiah saw that the entire temple was worshipping the Lord. His vision was a bit longer than others, but it was also precise and clear.

The visions of Jeremiah are similar to those of Amos. After calling Jeremiah, the Lord showed him two visions: "a branch of an almond tree" and "a boiling pot tilted away from the north."[35] In Jeremiah 24, the Lord showed Jeremiah a vision with a double meaning: "two baskets of figs placed before the temple of the Lord. . . . One basket had very good figs, . . . but the other basket

---

26. Exod 3:2–3.
27. 1 Kgs 22:17, 19.
28. Amos 7:1.
29. Amos 7:4.
30. Amos 7:7.
31. Amos 8:1.
32. Amos 9:1.
33. Isa 6:1.
34. Isa 6:2–4.
35. Jer 1:11, 13.

had very bad figs, so bad that they could not be eaten."³⁶ Later, the Lord showed Jeremiah "a vision of all the women remaining in the house of the king of Judah being led out to the officials of the king of Babylon."³⁷ Like the visions of Amos, the visions of Jeremiah are brief, precise, and about judgment.

In the two earlier vision stories in Ezekiel, the vision in one is specific, distinct, and identifiable; the vision in the other is complex, peculiar, and difficult to understand. In the first, the Lord, said Ezekiel, "set me down in the middle of a valley; it was full of bones. . . . [T]here were very many lying in the valley, and they were very dry."³⁸ The vision in this narrative is precise and recognizable, but the vision in Ezekiel 1 is altogether different. Walter Brueggemann called it "an enigmatic vision."³⁹ Following his declaration, "I saw visions of God,"⁴⁰ Ezekiel described four creatures, each with four faces and four wings; wheels within wheels by which the creatures could move in any direction; a crystal dome above the creatures; above the dome a throne; above the throne a human-like being; and a surrounding splendor.⁴¹ Then Ezekiel summarizes all he has seen: "This was the appearance (or sight or vision) of the likeness of the glory of the Lord."⁴² The question is: Is this vision earlier or apocalyptic? If we focus on Ezekiel's summary, we might consider it earlier; but it's hard to ignore the complexity and peculiarities of Ezekiel 1.

The New Testament accounts of earlier visions are also good illustrations of their precision, distinctness, and recognizability. With a few minor variations in words, the Synoptic Gospels agree that Jesus, following his baptism, saw the heaven opening and the Spirit descending on him like a dove.⁴³ With some variations in words they also agree that at the transfiguration of Jesus the

36. Jer 24:1–2.
37. Jer 38:22.
38. Ezek 37:1–2.
39. Brueggemann, *Introduction to the Old Testament*, 192.
40. Ezek 1:1.
41. Ezek 1:5–27.
42. Ezek 1:28.
43. Mark 1:10; Matt 3:16; Luke 3:21–22.

disciples saw a change in Jesus' physical appearance and clothing to a dazzling white and the appearance of Moses and Elijah in conversation with Jesus.[44]

The visions in Acts are similar. Acts 7 described Stephen's vision, "[H]e gazed into heaven and saw the glory of God and Jesus standing at the right hand of God."[45] All three accounts of Saul's conversion say Saul, on the road to Damascus saw "a light from heaven."[46] They differ only in their descriptions of the light's suddenness or brightness. The two accounts of Peter's vision are essentially the same. "He saw the heaven opened and something like a large sheet coming down, being lowered to the ground by its four corners. In it were all kinds of four-footed creatures and reptiles and birds."[47] And Paul saw "a man of Macedonia pleading with him and saying, 'Come over to Macedonia and help us.'"[48] Stephen, Paul, and Peter could describe or identify who or what they had actually seen.

Not every theophany or every use of the vocabulary of seeing is a vision story. The theophany at Mount Sinai is an example.[49] There is plenty of evidence that God was present at Mount Sinai: thunder, lightening, trumpet blasts, smoke, fire. The people of Israel met God there. There is also plenty of evidence of divine audition. God and Moses spoke with each other. But, there is no mention of vision in this story. Other than the presence of smoke and fire, neither Moses nor the people saw anything or anyone that they could specifically describe or identify. The narrative of Samuel's calling is another example. One of the story's opening lines says, "[V]isions were not widespread"; and toward its end, the story says, "Samuel was afraid to tell the vision to Eli."[50] The vocabulary of seeing frames the story, but there is no mention of

44. Mark 9:2–4; Matt 17:2–3; Luke 9:29–31.
45. Acts 7:55.
46. Acts 9:3; 22:6; 26:13.
47. Acts 10:11–12; cf. 11:5–6.
48. Acts 16:9.
49. Exod 19:16–25.
50. 1 Sam 3:1, 15.

vision. Neither Samuel nor Eli saw anything or anyone that they could describe or identify. A third example is the story of Elijah's encounter with the Lord at the cave entrance at Mount Horeb. Again, there is plenty of evidence the Lord was present—wind, earthquake, fire—but there was no vision, only a very quiet audition, "the sound of sheer silence."[51]

The specificity, distinctness, and identifiability of earlier visions do not mean they are devoid of all awe, wonder, or mystery. Who has never been awed at the sight of the Milky Way? Who wouldn't be curious about a blazing but unconsumed bush or a transfigured Jesus in conversation with Moses and Elijah? Who wouldn't be afraid at the sight of locusts swarming or a city's women and children being handed over to an enemy? Who wouldn't be inspired by the presence of God in the temple? Who wouldn't feel hope when bones live and persecutors see a "light from heaven"? The clarity and simplicity of these visions does not undermine their emotional power or reduce them to platitudes. If anything, their clarity and simplicity enhance their power and enrich them as metaphors for faith.

Direct and Unmediated

In the earlier vision stories, the vision is transmitted directly from God to its recipient(s). There are no intermediaries between God and the one(s) who saw the vision, not even in the long, complex vision in Ezekiel 1. At first glance, however, the story in Exodus 3 appears to be an exception; for the story introduces the burning bush with the words, "The angel of the Lord appeared to [Moses] in a flame of fire out of a bush."[52] If this angel or messenger had appeared again in the story, or if it had spoken with Moses, the vision might have become a mediated vision. As it is, this "angel of the Lord" never reappears in the story; and the phrase serves as a rhetorical device that points to the vision's divine origin.

51. 1 Kgs 19:11–12.
52. Exod 3:2.

The Bible's Earlier Vision Stories

The absence of intermediaries in the earlier vision stories distinguishes them from certain vision stories in postexilic latter prophets, dream stories, angelophanies, and most of the Bible's apocalyptic literature. The eight vision stories in Zechariah 1–6 are examples of postexilic vision stories. In each of the eight there is a "man" or "angel" or "an angel who talked with me" who explains and shows something to the prophet. According to Brueggemann, all eight stories "include a 'symbolic sighting' that is characteristically enigmatic, followed by an interpretive commentary."[53] The man, angel, or angel-who-talked-with-me, whoever he is, delivers the interpretive commentary at the end of each story. He clearly serves as an intermediary between God and Zechariah.

In dream stories there is often an interpreter, one who can explain the meaning of a perplexing dream to its recipient. Joseph rose to power in Egypt in part because of his ability to interpret dreams,[54] and Daniel gained a king's favor because he could interpret dreams and the "writing on the wall."[55] Joseph and Daniel were the intermediaries between God who sent the dreams and the dreams' recipients.

In angelophanies the angels or messengers are the intermediaries. God sends the angel with a message for the recipient. The recipient doesn't see God or a vision; she or he only sees the angel. In the foretelling of the birth of John the Baptist, Zechariah saw and spoke with an angel; he saw neither God nor a vision.[56] In the foretelling of Jesus' birth, Mary saw and spoke with the angel Gabriel, but not with God or about a vision.[57] The apocalyptic visions in Daniel 7–12 have more in common with dream stories and angelophanies than with our earlier vision stories.

The entire book of Revelation professes to be mediated revelation. Its opening sentence declares, "The revelation of Jesus Christ which God gave him to show his servants what must soon

---

53. Brueggemann, *Introduction to the Old Testament*, 252.
54. Gen 40–41.
55. Dan 2, 4–5.
56. Luke 1:5–20.
57. Luke 1:26–38.

take place; he made it known *by sending his angel to his servant John.*"⁵⁸ In his commentary on Revelation, Brian Blount said of this sentence:

> God does not operate directly with humans, but through appropriately designated intermediaries. That presence is symbolized here by the unidentified angel. He bridges the gap between the divine and human so that God's revelation can make its necessary move.⁵⁹

Throughout Revelation angels function as intermediaries, showing specific sights to John and relaying messages between God and John. Later in his commentary, Blount said of another passage, "God works via angelic proxy."⁶⁰ Blount's statement accurately describes the Apocalypse of John, but it's inaccurate with respect to the earlier vision stories. According to these stories God gives vision without go-betweens.

Summary

Most of the Bible's earlier vision stories use a vocabulary of seeing either to introduce a vision or as an integral part of the story. They depict a vision as a specific, distinct object, scene, event, or person that a recipient could recognize and describe; and in them a vision is transmitted directly from God to its recipient(s) without human or angelic intermediaries. These characteristics, taken together, distinguish these stories from dream stories, angelophanies, auditions, apocalyptic vision narratives, some theophanies, and other literary forms.

---

58. Rev 1:1 (emphasis added).
59. Blount, *Revelation*, 29–30.
60. Ibid., 141.

4

Challenging Contemporary Concepts about Vision

THE BIBLE'S EARLIER VISION stories call into question much that we believe and think we know about vision and visioning in contemporary organizations. They pose formidable challenges to our current concepts of vision in five areas. (1) Source(s): From whom or what does vision come? (2) Subjects: What is vision about? What is its subject matter? (3) Time perspectives: A vision is for or about what time period, future, present, or past? (4) Recipients: To whom is vision sent or given? (5) Purpose: For what purpose is vision sent or given? I will examine each challenge.

Source(s)

The Bible's earlier vision stories either assert or assume that God is the one and only source of vision.

The strongest and most explicit affirmations of vision's divine origin are the visions in Amos and Jeremiah that use the second pattern of the vocabulary of seeing, as in "The Lord showed me a vision."[1] Almost as explicit are those stories that, without using the second pattern, describe God as showing a vision to the recipient. Such stories include Abram's vision of the night sky, Moses'

---

1. Amos 7:1, 4, 7; 8:1; Jer 24:1; 38:21.

Old Man Dreaming

vision of the burning bush, the vision of Elisha's servant, Jeremiah's visions of the almond tree and "a boiling pot tilted away from the north," and Ezekiel's visions of "the glory of the Lord" and the valley of dry bones.[2]

The remaining earlier Old Testament vision stories so clearly imply vision's divine origin that no other explanation for vision's source is conceivable. Amos, for example, "saw the Lord standing beside the alter"; and Isaiah "saw the Lord sitting on a throne" in the temple.[3] In the Hebrew Scriptures one sees God only when God chooses to reveal God's self. So, the writers of Amos 9 and Isaiah 6, and today's readers, may easily suppose that God alone initiated the visions that Amos and Isaiah saw. The narrative of Micaiah ben Imlah's vision of Israel scattered on the mountains makes the same assumption. For the prophet's oath, "As the Lord lives, whatever the Lord says to me, that I will speak," precedes his vision; and a second vision similar to Isaiah's vision, "I saw the Lord sitting on his throne," follows it.[4]

In the New Testament's vision stories, the words used in the account of each vision or the story's details point to each vision's divine origin. Jesus at his baptism, Stephen before the enraged crowd, and Peter at prayer saw "heaven(s) opened"; and Saul on the road to Damascus saw "a light from heaven."[5] The use of the word "heaven" denotes the divine origin of these visions.

In the transfiguration story, Jesus led the three disciples to the high mountain. They did not originate the journey. They saw, but did not initiate, the transfiguring of Jesus' appearance and the appearance of Moses and Elijah with Jesus. They responded with awe and the desire to erect three tents. Their actions were the actions of those who believed they had seen visions from God. And Paul's vision of the Macedonian man took place after being "forbidden by the Holy Spirit to speak the word in Asia" and being forbidden

---

2. Gen 15:5; Exod 3:2; 2 Kgs 6:7; Jer 1:11, 13; Ezek 1:3, 28; Ezek 37:1.
3. Amos 9:1; Isa 6:1.
4. 1 Kgs 22:14, 19.
5. Mark 1:10; Acts 7:56, 10:11; 9:3.

by "the Spirit of Jesus" to enter Bethynia.[6] These details lead one to conclude that God was at work in these particular visions, either to teach the disciples about Jesus' identity or to direct the course of Paul's mission.

The Bible's earlier vision stories are not its only affirmations of visions' divine origin. Other Scripture texts, such as the following Old Testament texts, also assert that vision comes from God alone:

> Thus says the Lord of hosts: Do not listen to the words of the prophets who prophesy to you; they are deluding you. They speak visions of their own *minds*, not from the mouth of the Lord. They keep saying to those who despise the word of the Lord, "It shall be well with you."[7]

> Mortal, prophesy against the prophets of Israel who are prophesying; say to those who prophesy out of their own *imagination*: "Hear the word of the Lord!" Thus says the Lord God, Alas for the senseless prophets who follow their own spirit, and have seen nothing! They have envisioned falsehood and lying divination; they say, "says the Lord," when the Lord has not sent them, and yet they wait for the fulfillment of their word! As for you, mortal, set your face against the daughters of your people, who prophesy out of their own *imagination*; prophesy against them.[8]

The italicized words are translations of the Hebrew word for "heart." This word means far more than the vital organ that pumps blood and oxygen to the rest of the human body. It may also mean "seat of energy, inner person, seat of emotions, mood, will, mind, conscience, middle, or life."[9] Hebrew anthropology understood the heart to be the center of the human being. It is the core of human nature and of each individual, the center of what makes each person human.

When Jeremiah and Ezekiel criticized certain of their era's prophets for false vision, deception, and failing to heed God's word, they went beyond affirming visions' divine origin. They explicitly

6. Acts 16:6–7.
7. Jer 23:16–17a.
8. Ezek 13:2–3, 6, 17.
9. Koehler and Baumgartner, *Lexicon in Veteris Testamenti Libros*, 468–70.

said what is merely implicit in the vision stories, namely, that visions "from the heart," from the human center, are false visions. Visions cannot come from human beings, from a person or group, not even from humanity's core. Vision can only come from God. Without using the word "vision," Paul in his letter to the Galatians seems to agree with Jeremiah and Ezekiel. Following the customary epistolary introduction, Paul criticized the Galatians for having deserted the gospel of the grace of Christ.[10] Then he began a personal defense of his work as an apostle with these words:

> For I want you to know, brothers and sisters, that the gospel that was proclaimed by me is not of human origin; for I did not receive it from a human source, nor was I taught it, but I received it through a *revelation* of Jesus Christ.[11]

The word "revelation" refers to any disclosure of God or of divine truth, including auditions, visions, dreams, angelophanies, and other means of disclosure.[12] Paul, therefore, made a distinction between the divine disclosure that came to him "through a revelation of Jesus Christ" and anything "of a human origin" or "from a human source." He explicitly disavowed the human origins or sources of his proclamation in favor of divine disclosure. If we apply Paul's disavowal and affirmation to vision and visioning, a vision cannot come from human beings. It can only come from God.

Without a doubt the Bible's earlier vision stories and certain biblical texts challenge, and sometimes contradict, contemporary understandings of vision's origins. Of those who wrote on vision and visioning in secular organizations, Senge believed vision began within an individual human being who clarifies and deepens her or his personal vision; and Nanus asserted that it originates from organizational leaders' values, information, foresight, insight, imagination, and judgment. Although Kotter did not discuss vision's source, he did refer to a visioning process that includes a guiding coalition, the exercise of both the head and the heart, and the involvement of

---

10. Gal 1:1–10.
11. Gal 1:11–12.
12. Abbott-Smith, *Manual Greek Lexicon of the New Testament*, 50.

a group of people. In other words, he referred to signs of vision's human origins. Even Stacey, who believed visioning to be impossible, argued that strategic directions could emerge from what managers do, that is, from human effort. For all of these writers vision originates in the human heart, the human center. They do not understand it to have an external, much less a divine, source.[13]

The writers on vision and visioning in church organizations are only a modest improvement over their secular counterparts. They assert that vision comes from God alone, but the visioning processes they describe have more in common with secular processes than with the Bible's vision stories. Barna and Mancini agree that vision comes from God alone, but Barna limits vision to visionary pastors and outlines for them an "acquisition process" consisting of psychological self-assessment, sociological assessment, reassessment of one's prayer life, and outside counselors. And Mancini recommends exercises in organizational assessment and building a vision frame. Neither Swan's writing nor my earlier work deals with vision's source(s).[14] In fact, none of the writers surveyed, secular or church, examined the Bible's vision stories or biblical texts on vision. If they had, they would have discovered stories and texts that call into question today's widely held belief that vision comes from within each of us, stories and texts that declare the real source of vision to be divine and external to us.

Subjects

With respect to vision's subject(s), in contemporary secular organizations and institutions visions are almost always about the organization itself, the institution itself, or related subjects such as leadership or marketing. Church organizations, for better or worse, are similar to their secular counterparts. Even though Barna focused on the pastor's ministry, Mancini on congregations, Swan on philanthropic programs, and my earlier writing on a

13. See chapter 1.
14. See chapter 2.

denomination, the institutional church is the one common subject of almost all of our visions and vision statements; and institutional survival is frequently our subtext.

The subjects of the visions in the Bible's earlier vision stories are a conspicuous contrast to the single focus of visions in contemporary organizations. For the Bible's stories present a diversity of subjects and sometimes more than one subject in the same narrative. Sights from the natural world are common subjects of the Bible's visions. The subject of Abram's vision was the stars in the heavens, too numerous to count, no doubt a reference to the Milky Way.[15] The subjects shown to Amos included "forming locusts at the time the latter growth began to sprout" and "a basket of summer fruit."[16] "A branch of an almond tree" and "two baskets of figs" were subjects of Jeremiah's visions.[17] In Jesus' post-baptism vision, he saw the Spirit "descending like a dove."[18] "A light from heaven" was the subject of Saul's vision, and a variety of unkosher animals was the subject of Peter's vision.[19]

Various forms of judgment, subjects definitely not found in contemporary visions, are also common among the Bible's visions. "All Israel scattered on the mountains" was the subject of Micaiah ben Imlah's first vision.[20] "Forming locusts," "a judgment by fire," and "a plumb line" were subjects of Amos' visions.[21] The almond tree branch, "a boiling pot, tilted away from the north," "two baskets of figs," and the women "being led out to the officials of the king of Babylon" were subjects of Jeremiah's visions.[22] As these vision subjects clearly illustrate, there is no guarantee that visions from God will always be positive or pleasant. God can call us to

---

15. Gen 15:5.
16. Amos 7:1; 8:1.
17. Jer 1:11; 24:1.
18. Matt 3:16; Mark 1:10; Luke 3:22.
19. Acts 9:3; 22:6; 26:13; 10:12.
20. 1 Kgs 22:17.
21. Amos 7:1, 4, 7.
22. Jer 1:11, 13; 24:1; 38:22.

account for any unrighteousness, whether great or small; and God may certainly do so through a vision.

Sometimes God as God is the subject of the Bible's visions. Micaiah ben Imlah's second vision was of the Lord on his throne enticing King Ahab into destruction.[23] "The Lord standing beside the alter," "the Lord sitting on a throne" in the temple, and "the glory of the Lord" were the subjects of Amos', Isaiah's, and Ezekiel's visions, respectively.[24]

Sometimes Jesus is the subject of the Bible's visions. Following his baptism he saw the Spirit descending on him.[25] He was both the subject and the recipient of the vision. In the transfiguration story he was the one whose appearance was transfigured and the one seen with Moses and Elijah. In Stephen's vision he was the one seen "at the right hand of God."[26]

In some cases vision's subject seems to be unique to a particular story. A bush ablaze, but not consumed, "the mountain . . . full of horses and chariots of fire all around Elisha," the valley of dry bones, and "the man of Macedonia" are examples of singular subjects.[27] They illustrate the diversity of subjects found among the Bible's visions.

God does not limit visions to organizational or institutional maintenance or progress. In fact, none of the Bible's visions are about organizations or institutions. Instead their subjects are multiple and multifaceted, far richer in content than anything found in typical administrative processes, bureaucracy, or vision statements.

---

23. 1 Kgs 22:19–20.
24. Amos 9:1; Isa 6:1; Ezek 1:28.
25. Matt 3:16; Mark 1:10; Luke 3:21–22.
26. Acts 7:55–56.
27. Exod 3:2; 2 Kgs 6:17; Ezek 37:1–2; Acts 16:9.

Time Perspectives

"What's your definition of vision?" asked a friend. Then he answered his own question: "The common definition is future." As my friend said, most people believe that vision is about the future, about a future state, future conditions, or a future destination; and writers on vision and visioning in secular organizations have adopted this prevailing opinion. They define vision as a picture of the future or an organizational destination. Even Stacey, who argues that the future is unknowable, acknowledges that one concept of vision is vision as a future state or destination.[28] Moreover, our writers on vision and visioning in church organizations have also adopted the prevailing view. They too believe or assume that vision is about the future.[29]

But is it? Is vision always about the future, always about a future state, future circumstances, or a future destination? In my experience the answer is no. There are from time to time visions about the present and even about the past. We humans, through our use of experience, observation, and some imagination, do occasionally envision a present state or conditions or a past state or conditions. The boundaries between past and present and present and future are flexible, not rigid and limiting.

In my pre-retirement years I often observed, organized, participated in, and led meetings. Occasionally it was my good fortune to work with meeting participants who had a remarkable ability to "see" what was happening around them. They could listen carefully, ask a few questions, and then visualize problems or circumstances so clearly that they enhanced a group's understanding of the issues before them. Although no one described it this way, they envisioned the present; and their insights were extraordinarily valuable to a group and to its productivity.

In some of my continuing education I worked with other clergy and a group of family therapists. We often examined case studies from our own lives and work; and as a participant in the discussion of those studies, I frequently marveled at the ability of

---

28. See chapter 1.
29. See chapter 2.

my colleagues and teachers to see the ongoing human dynamics in those situations. They could visualize what I, at first, could not. Again, although no one described it this way, they envisioned the present; and by doing so, others and I gradually learned that we too could envision what was happening around us. These illustrations are merely glimpses of vision's unlimited time perspectives. Vision can be about the present as well as about the future.

Vision can also be about the past, although it may at first seem counterintuitive. I was once invited to a lecture given by a historian, a professor at an Ivy League university. The professor's specialty was the history of ideas. As he lectured, he described the presence and the absence of certain ideas in American society since about 1970. By the end of his lecture, the audience and I had a much clearer understanding of the last forty to fifty years of U.S. history. The professor had envisioned for us our recent past. He gave us a new way of seeing and understanding our own history.

In my continuing education with clergy and family therapists, each participant learned to envision her or his own family's history. This does not mean that we had license to create our family's story out of nothing. Far from it. Our histories were based on hard data (dates, names, places, etc.) and on accounts of personal contacts and relationships with family members, and they required research on our part. We envisioned our past in that each of us learned new ways of seeing our families and ourselves.

Our human experience, however, is not the only basis for saying that vision is not always about the future. For the Bible's earlier visions are usually about the present, not the future, by which I mean that visions' recipients understood that they were seeing specific objects, scenes, events, or people in a time contemporaneous with their own. They were not seeing something or someone in a time to come.

Although we should not assume that the Bible's earlier visions are always about the future, neither should we assume that they are always about the present. Most of the Bible's visions about the present have future implications or consequences that appear later in each story. Also, some of the Bible's earlier visions really are about the future; but it's always a foreseeable future, not a distant future. Micaiah ben Imlah's visions and Jeremiah's vision of the women "being led out to the officials of the king of Babylon" are examples of visions about the future.[30] One vision even refers to the past, namely, the appearance of Moses and Elijah talking with Jesus in the transfiguration story. The point is that the Bible's visions are not limited to one time perspective. They seem to roam across the chronological spectrum of past, present, and future.

Recipients

Writers on vision in secular organizations imply that organizational leaders and managers are a vision's recipients.[31] Within church organizations, Barna said pastors are a vision's recipients, Mancini implied that missional leaders are its recipients, and Swan identified vision as a talent or ability of those who start or transform philanthropic programs.[32] All of these recipients have one characteristic in common: their organizational or institutional connections. All are recipients of an organization's vision because they are leaders, employees, or members of that organization.

In contrast, the Bible's earlier visions were never given to a person on the basis of his or her organizational leadership, employment, or membership. They were given instead by God's grace and by God's choice and often given to those whom we might consider unlikely and even unworthy.

The Bible's list of vision recipients looks like a roll call of the faith's heroes, a veritable who's who of biblical characters. But what if our record of their lives and work were limited to the period prior to the receipt of their first vision? Would we then consider them likely recipients of visions from God? We might not, for the record of their earlier lives often shows them to have been less than

---

30. 1 Kgs 22:17, 19; Jer 38:22.
31. See chapter 1.
32. See chapter 2.

heroic or promising and not necessarily organizationally or institutionally connected.

Abram, for example, had been called by God to go from his country, his kindred, and his father's house.[33] He became God's "wandering Aramean,"[34] not necessarily a sign of a great nation to come. Moses murdered an Egyptian and fled to the land of Midian to escape Pharaoh's just punishment.[35] Micaiah had already earned the king's hatred. "He never prophesies anything favorable about me," said King Ahab.[36] Amos "was among the shepherds of Tekoa,"[37] and he disavowed any connection with the prophets of his day. "I am no prophet, nor a prophet's son: but I am a herdsman, and a dresser of sycamore trees," he said.[38] We know very little about Isaiah's early life, but the traditional view is that he "was an upper class Jerusalemite who was part of the city's central social structure but not necessarily a part of its religious establishment."[39] Immediately after God's call and before his first visions, Jeremiah complained, "I do not know how to speak, for I am only a boy,"[40] a complaint God answered with a promise of divine presence and additional instructions.[41] And Ezekiel was "among the exiles,"[42] one of those sent to Babylon in the first deportation in about 597 BCE. He was a displaced person in a foreign context, a person forcibly disconnected from his religious institutions in Jerusalem.

The New Testament's vision recipients are similar to those in the Old Testament. Jesus called Peter, James, and John to leave their nets and become his first disciples. They saw the transfiguration of Jesus because Jesus took them with him to the mountain. Jesus

33. Gen 12:1.
34. Deut 26:5.
35. Exod 2:11–22.
36. 1 Kgs 22:8.
37. Amos 1:1.
38. Amos 7:14.
39. Wilson, *Prophecy and Society in Ancient Israel*, 271.
40. Jer 1:6.
41. Jer 1:8–10.
42. Ezek 1:1.

chose them to accompany him.⁴³ Stephen, one of seven originally appointed to serve tables, was seized and brought before the Jewish council.⁴⁴ He addressed the council so strongly that they became enraged. He was definitely not one of the Jewish establishment's leaders.⁴⁵ Saul, called Paul, approved the stoning of Stephen; persecuted the church in Jerusalem; committed Christians to prison; and received letters from the high priest to go to Damascus, arrest Christians, and send them to Jerusalem for punishment.⁴⁶ He was part of the Jewish institutional establishment; and before his conversion, there was no reason to believe that he would ever be a Christian or a church leader. Peter's vision of the unkosher animals challenged the very practices he had been following.

None of those who received one of the Bible's earlier visions did so because of their organizational membership or leadership or because they were likely or worthy to receive. They received it by God's grace and God's choice alone.

Purpose: Vision as Pointer and Preparation

In a book chapter titled "The Prophet's Call and Reception of Revelation," Gerhard von Rad made two provocative statements on the purpose of visions given to the prophets:

> The purpose of the vision was not to impart knowledge of higher worlds. It was intended to open the prophet's eyes to coming events which were not only of a spiritual sort, but were also to be concrete realities in the objective world.⁴⁷

> A revelation . . . can never have been an end in itself. Least of all was it given to the prophet to let him know that God was near him. Its purpose was to equip him for his office.⁴⁸

43. Matt 17:1; Mark 9:2; Luke 9:28.
44. Acts 6:2, 12.
45. Acts 7:51–53.
46. Acts 8:1–3; 9:1–2.
47. Rad, *Old Testament Theology*, 59.
48. Ibid., 63.

The key phrases, I believe, are "to open the prophet's eyes" and "to equip him for his office." These two phrases summarize the purposes of the visions given to the prophets. Either they were given to point the prophets toward realities not yet recognized, or they were given to prepare them for the calling and work ahead of them. In some cases a vision served both purposes. In my opinion, von Rad's statements apply to the purposes of most of the Bible's earlier visions.

In order to discern the purpose of the Bible's earlier visions, I recommend that readers pay close attention to the dialogue and events that follow (and sometimes precede) a vision's appearance in a vision story. Scholars have long noted that visions are frequently followed by auditions.[49] These auditions, and other events following a vision, usually point a vision's recipient toward a not-yet-recognized reality, or they prepare the recipient for the calling and work ahead. In so doing, they identify a vision's purpose.

Micaiah ben Imlah's first vision of "Israel scattered on the mountains" verified what the kings of Judah and Israel suspected, namely, that Micaiah knew that the impending war would end in disaster. The purpose of his second vision, a vision of how God allowed the enticement of King Ahab by putting lying spirits in the mouths of Ahab's prophets, became clear in the words that followed. "The Lord has decreed disaster for you,"[50] said the prophet to the two kings.[51]

As noted previously, Amos' visions were about judgment, but they differed somewhat in their specific purposes. The purpose of Amos' first two visions, visions of forming locusts and of God calling for a shower of fire, was to point to the massive and indiscriminate devastation that God's judgment would bring. So extensive would the devastation of famine and fire have been, that the prophet himself opened conversation with God with the plea, "O Lord God, cease, I beg you! How can Jacob stand? He is so small!"[52] God heard Amos' plea and relented. The purpose of Amos' next two visions,

49. Ibid., 59.
50. 1 Kgs 22:23.
51. Cf. Park, "Story, Interpretation, and Identity," 5–7.
52. Amos 7:2, 5.

visions of a plumb line and a basket of summer fruit, was to point to more discriminate and less destructive forms of judgment that would befall Israel. Following these two visions God, not Amos, initiated the conversation; first, to point to his "setting a plumb line in the midst of . . . Israel," a metaphor for establishing a way of measuring and judging Israel's "sanctuaries" and its rulers;[53] and second, to point, through a play on the similarity of the Hebrew words for "fruit" and "end,"[54] to the coming end of Israel as a nation-state. Judgment is still judgment even if less destructive.

The purpose of Jeremiah's first two visions, the vision of an almond tree branch, with its play on the similarity of the Hebrew words for "almond tree" and "watching," and the vision of a boiling pot in the north, was to prepare the prophet for God's impending judgment and for the difficulty of the prophetic task to come.[55]

The purpose of Jeremiah's vision of the baskets of good and bad figs was to point to the two different futures that God's people would experience. The two auditions following the vision describe each future.[56] Ironically, the exiles, those sent to Babylon in the first deportation, were promised God's favor, eventual return to their land, rebuilding, and restoration of the covenant relationship. In contrast, the government in Jerusalem and those who remained in Jerusalem or were sent to Egypt were promised eventual destruction.

The purposes of the New Testament's earlier visions are similar to those in the Old, and the auditions or events immediately following (and sometimes preceding) each vision are usually keys to each vision's purpose. For example, a voice from heaven saying, "You are my Son, the Beloved; with you I am well pleased,"[57] follows Jesus' vision of "the Spirit descending like a dove on him" after his baptism. The purpose of the vision, therefore, was to identify Jesus as God's Son.

---

53. Amos 7:8–9.
54. Amos 8:2–3.
55. Jer 1:11–19.
56. Jer 24:4–10.
57. Mark 1:11.

Sometimes an audition following a vision not only identifies the vision's purpose, but also extends and deepens its purpose. For example, immediately after Abram's vision of innumerable stars in the night sky, God said to Abram, "So shall your descendants be."[58] From this sentence we can discern that the purpose of the vision was to point Abram to God's promise to make Abram's descendants also innumerable. The remainder of the audition extends the purpose, and our understanding of it, by including Abram's faithful response to God's promise, God's counting Abram's belief "as righteousness," God's promise of land, and the making of a covenant between God and Abram.[59]

The story of Ezekiel's vision of the valley of dry bones is similar to the story of Abram's vision of stars in the night sky. The purpose of Ezekiel's vision was to point to God's promise to breathe new life into Israel's dead bones, a promise that exiles needed to hear; but the dialogue between God and the prophet did not end with God's promise. It continued to the opening of "graves," a potential allusion to the resurrection of the dead and to restoration of Israel in its own land.[60]

Even the transfiguration stories appear to go a step beyond the purpose of their visions. The purpose of the visions in the transfiguration stories resembles the purpose in the baptism stories. A voice from an overshadowing cloud saying, "This is my Son, the Beloved; listen to him!"[61] follows the visions of Jesus' changed appearance and of Moses and Elijah talking with Jesus. Thus, the purpose of the two visions was to point to Jesus as God's Son, as the one whom God sent and is sending to us and for us. As if to emphasize this point, all three Synoptic writers used the identical Greek phrase in the closing sentence of their transfiguration stories, a phrase that means "Jesus only" or "Jesus alone."[62] In using

---

58. Gen 15:5.
59. Gen 15:6–18.
60. Ezek 37:12–14.
61. Mark 9:7.
62. Mark 9:8; Matt 17:8; Luke 9:36.

this phrase the writers seemed to underscore the christological purpose of the transfiguration visions.

Visions in the longer vision stories and in stories for which there are multiple accounts sometimes serve two kinds of purposes for their recipient(s): immediate or short-term purposes, and longer-term or extended-duration purposes. The longer-term purposes are frequently theologically significant and often overshadow the visions that set them in motion.

Moses' vision of the burning bush seems to have had two short-term purposes: (1) to get Moses' attention and (2) to reveal the holiness of God. Moses' initial statement in response to the vision points to the first: "I must turn aside and look at this great sight, and see why the bush is not burned up."[63] God's command to Moses in response to his turning aside points to the second: "Come no closer! Remove the sandals from your feet, for the place on which you are standing is holy ground."[64] This initial dialogue between Moses and God was the beginning of one of the most remarkable auditions in the Bible, an audition that then revealed two long-range purposes for the vision: (1) to prepare Moses for a call to go "to Pharaoh to bring my people, the Israelites, out of Egypt,"[65] a call to go to one of the world's most powerful rulers to obtain the freedom of people enslaved and oppressed by that ruler, and to lead them to another land; and (2) to prepare Moses to "name," to identify, the God who called him. "I AM WHO I AM," or, as James Muilenburg suggested, "I CAUSE TO HAPPEN WHAT HAPPENS," said God to Moses.[66] "Say to the Israelites, 'I AM (or I CAUSE TO HAPPEN) has sent me to you.'"[67]

The short-term purpose of Isaiah's vision of God on a throne in the temple was twofold: (1) to reveal to Isaiah God's holiness, as indicated by the hymn, "Holy, holy, holy";[68] and (2) to prepare

63. Exod 3:3.
64. Exod 3:5.
65. Exod 3:10.
66. Muilenburg, *Way of Israel*, 44–45.
67. Exod 3:13–14.
68. Isa 6:3.

Challenging Contemporary Concepts about Vision

the prophet for his own confession of unworthiness and God's declaration of pardon.[69] The confession and pardon opened a conversation between God and Isaiah, a conversation that brought out the long-range purpose of God's self-revelation to Isaiah. "Whom shall I send," asked God, "and who will go for us?" Isaiah responded to the call, "Here am I, send me!"[70] The rest of the story suggests that the prophet was called to preach to a people who would not hear, see, or even understand God's message to and for them.[71] Only in the story's final sentence, "The holy seed is its stump," did Isaiah hear a glimmer of hope and grace about his task.[72]

Ezekiel's vision of the glory of God is somewhat similar to Moses' and Isaiah's visions. Its purpose was to prepare him to receive God's call to be a prophet among the people in exile.[73] In the long dialogue between God and Ezekiel that followed the vision, God gradually revealed to the prophet, one component at a time, the difficulty of his task.[74]

The purpose of Saul's vision on the road to Damascus was to get his attention, to point him in a different direction toward Jesus, and to prepare him for a new life to come. The three accounts of Saul's vision in Acts agree on the sequence of events immediately following the vision. The light from heaven knocked Saul off his feet. A voice said to him, "Saul, why do you persecute me?" He asked, "Who are you, Lord?" The voice answered, "I am Jesus, whom you are persecuting."[75] In this brief conversation Jesus, the one whom Saul had rejected, confronted him and challenged his behavior as a persecutor. The three accounts differ, however, over who specifically transmitted the call and task from God to Paul. Johannes Munck summarized the differences when he wrote, "In the accounts in Acts, Christ speaks either directly to Paul (ch. 26),

---

69. Isa 6:5–7.
70. Isa 6:8.
71. Isa 6:9–13a.
72. Isa 6:13b.
73. Ezek 2:1–7.
74. Ezek 2–3.
75. Acts 9:4–5.

or through Ananias (ch. 22), or to Ananias (ch. 9)."[76] Munck also called attention to a fourth account, Paul's own account in Galatians 1:15–16, an account that says nothing about the vision on the road to Damascus, who transmitted the call from God to Paul, or what was said in the transmission thereof.[77]

Although the four accounts differ in the details of Paul's call, they agree unanimously that God called Paul to the task of presenting the good news of Jesus Christ to the Gentiles. Paul was specifically chosen to cross the religious and cultural boundaries between Jews and Gentiles and to become a "witness to all people."[78]

The vision stories in Acts are noteworthy for their long-term mission purposes. Consider Stephen's vision of "Jesus standing at the right hand of God."[79] His address before the Jewish council enraged the council; and in the midst of their rage, the vision appeared. In this setting the vision validated Stephen's Christian faith. It clearly associated Jesus with God and made visible the very thing the Jewish council did not want to believe. It then led, with Saul's approval, to the stoning of Stephen[80] and to the persecution, imprisonment, and scattering of believers throughout Judea and Samaria.[81]

But the scattering of believers is not the end of the story. Philip, one of the scattered, preached and healed in Samaria and even baptized an Ethiopian eunuch. Stephen's vision set in motion a sequence of events that spread the gospel to new geographic areas, people, and cultures.[82]

The purpose of Peter's vision of the descending sheet with "all kinds of four-footed creatures and reptiles and birds of the air" was to point Peter to the possibility of breaking through the cultural, social, and religious barriers between Jews and Gentiles. This purpose came into focus in the audition following the vision. A voice

76. Munck, *Paul and the Salvation of Mankind*, 24.
77. Ibid., 24–26.
78. Acts 22:15.
79. Acts 7:56.
80. Acts 7:58—8:1a.
81. Acts 8:1b–3.
82. Acts 8:4–8, 14–17, 25–40.

challenged Peter's kosher keeping with the words, "Get up, Peter; kill and eat." Peter asserted his good Jewish practice, "By no means, Lord; for I have never eaten anything that is profane or unclean." The voice then alluded to the creation narratives in which God had made all things good, "What God has made clean, you must not call profane."[83] The rest of the story recounts Peter's ministry to a Gentile, Cornelius, and the beginning of mission to the Gentiles.

Paul's vision of a man of Macedonia was clearly a call to spread the gospel from Asia to Europe, to expand the reach of Christianity from one continent to many continents. When Paul and his companions "tried to cross over to Macedonia,"[84] they confirmed this vision's purpose.

The Bible's earlier visions are never ends in themselves. They always point to, prepare for, or confirm something else. And the Bible's earlier visions are not destinations toward which we are moving. Instead they are points of departure given by God to point to what God is saying or doing or promising to do in the lives of visions' recipient(s) and among God's people. In contrast to visions in contemporary organizations, the Bible's earlier visions are not limited to organizational or institutional concerns. They serve instead the purposes of the God who was, is, and shall be creator, redeemer, and sustainer of all.

Observations and Questions

According to the Bible's earlier vision stories, God showed visions to particular individuals. But, in observing that the recipients of the earlier visions were individuals, I am not arguing that the effects of these visions were limited to private, personal, individualistic, or non-communal spheres of faith and life. Just as I noted previously that visions seen in present time might have implications for the future, so I would also note that visions given to individuals might

---

83. Acts 10:13–15.
84. Acts 16:10.

have implications for the nation, the people of God, the community of faith, the body of Christ.

The earlier vision stories themselves attest to a variety of social, political, or communal implications, even though the visions' recipients were particular people. Abram's vision of stars in the night sky preceded God's promises of innumerable descendents and of land, two promises with enormous ramifications for future generations. Moses was called to "bring [God's] people, the Israelites, out of Egypt,"[85] a political act that affected both the Egyptians and the Israelites. Micaiah ben Imlah "saw all Israel scattered on the mountain, like sheep that have no shepherd"[86]; Amos saw " a basket of summer fruit" signifying "the end" of the "people Israel"[87]; and Jeremiah saw "a boiling pot tilted away from the north."[88] These three visions referred to judgment that would befall the entire nation. Following his call Ezekiel was made "a sentinel," a watchman, "for the house of Israel"[89]; and at the valley of dry bones God promised to bring the people "back to the land of Israel."[90] These two actions buttressed the spirits of the people in exile in Babylon. And how can we ignore the role that Stephen's, Paul's, and Peter's visions played in energizing mission in the early church? An individual's receipt of a vision does not eliminate or lessen the vision's social, political, or communal consequences.

We should also observe that the earlier visions are logically secondary to God's purposes, even when they appear chronologically first in the vision stories. If visions are secondary to God's purposes, then for Christians the most important questions are not: What's our vision? Show us your vision statement! What do we foresee for next year or for the next decade? For us there are deeper, more profound and more challenging questions. Such questions are foundational questions that look beyond what we

85. Exod 3:10.
86. 1 Kgs 22:17.
87. Amos 8:2.
88. Jer 1:13.
89. Ezek 3:17.
90. Ezek 37:12.

see to the source of our seeing. Ultimately, they are questions of trust. Do we really trust the one living God who creates, redeems, and sustains the world and us, the God revealed in Jesus Christ?

Based on the earlier vision stories generally, we might reframe our questions of trust as follows: Will we trust the one God who is the source, the origin, of all vision? Do we trust the living God who shows us far more than administrative processes or institutional maintenance, even uncomfortable things like judgment? Will we trust the God of all time, the God whose visions have roamed across the chronological spectrum of past, present, and future? Can we trust the God who graciously chooses to send visions to those whom we might consider unlikely or unworthy recipients? Should we trust God to prepare us for new realities and new adventures?

And based on specific vision stories, we might frame specific questions of trust: Do we trust the God who showed Abram the night sky to give us, when we are in pain or anguish, a faith sufficient to survive the dark nights of our souls? Will we trust God to hear our and the world's cries and to accompany us when we are sent to our contemporary social, economic, or political Pharaohs? In a world where much is monetized, quantified, and materialistically reduced, do we believe that our God causes to happen what happens, that our God really is the Lord of history?[91] Can we trust a God who might give us an impossible task, cause us to consume indigestible "words of mourning and woe,"[92] or uproot us and send us to an alien land? Is God's promise to breathe new life into our dead bones even credible in a time when everything seems to be falling apart? In a culture of religious pluralism, what does it mean to see "only Jesus"? With cultural and racial diversity surrounding us, could God be calling us, and our congregations, to cross religious boundaries in our communities in order to become a "witness to all people"?[93] The Bible's earlier vision stories invite us to grapple with these questions.

91. Muilenburg, *Way of Israel*, 45.
92. Ezek 2:10.
93. Acts 22:18.

5

Expanding Perspectives: More Texts about Vision

IN ADDITION TO EARLIER vision stories, other texts about vision appear in the Bible. These texts do not conform to particular patterns like those found in earlier vision stories. Many do not use a vocabulary of seeing; and most do not describe or mention any particular vision, although vision or a related topic is clearly the subject of each text. Many are also not stories, but other forms of literature. Several are prophetic oracles. One is a teaching or saying of Jesus, and one is a proverb. These other texts enlarge and enrich our understanding of biblical concepts of and perspectives on vision. They supplement the earlier vision stories; and in so doing they give us a more robust understanding of vision and its purposes among God's people.

Seer and Seen: God and Hagar

The stories about Hagar in Genesis 16 and 21 appear at first to say nothing about vision. They begin with two facts: (1) after approximately ten years of marriage, Sarai, Abram's wife, had borne him no children; and (2) Sarai owned an Egyptian slave-girl named Hagar.[1] As a slave, Hagar had no economic, political, or social

---

1. Gen 16:1.

rights. She was subject to Sarai's complete authority; and although she was in and around Sarai's family daily, she was not considered a family member and did not enjoy the family privileges of inheritance, property ownership, or a voice in decisions. She was, as her story was about to reveal, a powerless "other," a pawn in the plan of her mistress Sarai.

Sarai, meanwhile, was preoccupied with her lack of children. How could God "make of Abram a great nation"[2] without her bearing children? So, Sarai devised her own plan to fulfill God's promise. She blamed God for preventing her from bearing children and proposed to Abram that Hagar become her surrogate and bear Abram's children. With Abram's consent, Sarai then gave Hagar to Abram to become a surrogate mother; and from their sexual union Hagar became pregnant. But Sarai's plan had unintended consequences. When Hagar recognized that she was pregnant, she "looked with contempt" upon Sarai, who was no doubt jealous and blamed Abram for Hagar's contempt, to which Abram said to Sarai, "Your slave-girl is in your power: do to her as you please."[3] After twice blaming someone else for her misfortune, and Abram's denial of responsibility in this matter, Sarai dealt harshly with Hagar; and Hagar ran away. Sarai's best laid plan had gone awry.

Despite Hagar's flight, a messenger from God found her in the wilderness. Note at this point that God's messenger sought Hagar, the powerless slave-girl. Hagar was not seeking God. When the messenger asked her where she had come from and where she was going, Hagar admitted that she was running away from Sarai. Then the messenger delivered to her three messages: a command, "Return to your mistress"; a promise, "I will so multiply your offspring that they cannot be counted"; and the name of her child, "You . . . shall bear a son; you shall call him Ishmael, for the Lord has given heed to your affliction."[4] The name Ishmael means "God hears." God had chosen to shower divine grace on this powerless slave, on one who had not

---

2. Gen 12:2.
3. Gen 16:6.
4. Gen 16:7–11.

requested such grace and who, in Abram's and Sarai's household, would have been thought unworthy to receive such grace.

Genesis 16:13 is Hagar's response to God's graciousness. Although 16:13 does not describe or mention any particular vision, it uses a vocabulary of seeing and reinforces some of the concepts about vision found in the earlier vision stories. Grammatically it is one sentence with two main clauses joined by a conjunction meaning "for" or "because." The second clause is therefore a rationale for the first. Both clauses pose challenges to biblical translators and interpreters. A literal translation of the first clause from Hebrew into English says of Hagar: "She called the name of Yahweh who spoke to her, 'You are El-roi.'" El-roi means "God of seeing" or "God who sees" or possibly "God is seeing." Somewhat like Moses in Exodus 3, Hagar named or identified the God who had spoken to her through a messenger. This God, El-roi, was not an aloof, abstract being, but the God of seeing, the One who sees, the ultimate seer. To reiterate this point in words used in the previous chapter, the slave-girl Hagar identified God as the source or origin of all vision.

But from what did Hagar derive the name El-roi? The second clause in 16:13 is supposed to answer this question. Unfortunately, there are both textual and translation problems in the Hebrew text of this clause. Because the New International Version's (NIV) translation of the second clause adheres to the basic meanings of the Hebrew words in the clause and because it communicates clearly the apparent intent of the clause, I recommend we follow it. It reads, "For she said, 'I have now seen the One who sees me.'" As the unlikely recipient of God's promise to multiply her offspring and God's mercy in paying heed to her affliction, Hagar understood herself to have seen God and to have been seen by God, to have seen and been seen by the One who could break through her social and economic chains. Hagar named God El-roi because she had seen and been seen by the God who sees.

Hagar's story continued in Genesis 21. Abram and Sarai have been renamed Abraham and Sarah. Hagar gave birth to Ishmael, and Sarah gave birth to Isaac. Ishmael and Isaac were playmates. When Sarah saw the two boys playing together, she asked Abraham

Expanding Perspectives: More Texts about Vision

to cast out Hagar because, as she said, "The son of this slave woman shall not inherit along with my son Isaac."[5] This request distressed Abraham, but God assured him that his offspring would be recognized through Isaac and that Ishmael's offspring would become a nation. So Abraham gave Hagar a supply of food and water and sent her and Ishmael away.[6] When they ran out of food and water, Hagar left Ishmael under a bush and walked some distance away from the bush because she did not want to "look on the death of the child."[7] At this point God intervened. God's messenger instructed Hagar to pick up Ishmael, and he repeated the promise to "make a great nation of him."[8] "Then God opened her eyes and she saw a well of water. She went, and filled the skin with water, and gave the boy a drink."[9] God had again "opened [Hagar's] eyes."

Walter Brueggemann observed that mothers in Genesis played an important role in the faith tradition and that feminist interpreters have called special attention to the positive place of Hagar in the tradition. Brueggemann wrote:

> Hagar embodies the fidelity of God to the family of faith that persists just outside the primal genealogy of Abraham, Isaac, and Jacob. She functions in the narrative to keep the horizon of Israel open to "the other" who also has legitimate claims to make upon the promise of God. Her presence in the tradition precludes the excessive narrowing of the tradition.[10]

Brueggemann added, "The mothers of the family are valued, but then so is Hagar, who lives at the edge of the family of choice."[11]

With respect to vision, however, Hagar's story does more than " preclude the excessive narrowing of the tradition." It implies that no one, not even a powerless slave-girl, is outside the scope of

---

5. Gen 21:10.
6. Gen 21:14.
7. Gen 21:16.
8. Gen 21:18.
9. Gen 21:19.
10. Brueggemann, *Introduction to the Old Testament*, 50.
11. Ibid., 51.

God's vision or the range of God's grace. It strongly suggests that the one "at the edge of the family of choice" may indeed see the God who sees.

A Vision of Things to Come

Isaiah 2:2–4 and Micah 4:1–3 are two versions of the same vision. The differences between them are insignificant. Isaiah 2:1 introduces this vision using a vocabulary of seeing: "The word that Isaiah son of Amoz *saw* concerning Judah and Jerusalem." And Micah 4:4 adds three lines to this vision, lines not found in Isaiah's version. The consensus among scholars regarding the origin of this vision and its two versions has been that we have "a passage of anonymous origin which was at one time attributed to Isaiah and at another to Micah."[12]

If the origin of this vision is unknown, the vision itself is one of the clearest and most compelling in the Bible. The vision opens by identifying its time perspective: "In days to come . . ."[13] This vision is intentionally about the future. It envisions the mountain of God's house, the temple mount, Mount Zion, being elevated above other hills and mountains. "All the nations shall stream to it."[14] People and nations will come and say, "Let us go up to the mountain of the Lord, to the house of the God of Jacob; that he may teach us his ways and that we may walk in his paths."[15] Instruction will come out of Zion and the word of the Lord from Jerusalem. God will judge between people and arbitrate between nations. Then "they shall beat their swords into plowshares and their spears into pruning hooks; nation shall not lift up sword against nation, neither shall they learn war any more."[16]

---

12. Eissfeldt, *Old Testament*, 318.
13. Isa 2:2; Mic 4:1.
14. Isa 2:2; Mic 4:1.
15. Isa 2:3; Mic 4:2.
16. Isa 2:4; Mic 4:3.

Expanding Perspectives: More Texts about Vision

This is a glorious vision of hope: the prominence of God's house; the pilgrimage of all nations to receive God's instructions and word; God's righteous judging and arbitration; and the resulting peace and absence of war, arms, and violence. Note that God's teaching and God's judging and arbitration precede and are the precondition for peace and the absence of violence. Note also that this vision is not for or about particular individuals; it is for and about people, nations, the community of nations, and the community of the faithful.

Micah adds to this glorious vision. People and nations "shall sit under their own vines and . . . fig trees, and no one shall make them afraid."[17] To peace and the absence of war, Micah adds agricultural well-being and the absence of fear. Micah concludes by identifying God as the source of this vision: "The mouth of the Lord of hosts has spoken."

Walter Brueggemann compared this vision's understanding of the temple with the understanding in a passage from Isaiah 56:

> These [foreigners and eunuchs] I will bring to my holy mountain,
>   and make them joyful in my house of prayer;
> their burnt offerings and sacrifices
>   will be accepted on my altar;
> for my house shall be called a house of prayer
>   for all peoples.[18]

Said Brueggemann, "The poetry anticipates inclusive worship in the Jerusalem temple and evokes the now-familiar phrase, 'a house of prayer for all peoples.'"[19]

But questions remain. Who were or are the recipients of this glorious vision of hope? What was or is its purpose? Neither Isaiah 2 nor Micah 4 answer definitively. They speak instead of matters other than identification of this vision's recipients or its purpose. They bear witness to the God who opens his house in hospitality to all comers, the God who invites and receives all people from every

---

17. Mic 4:4.
18. Isa 56:7.
19. Brueggemann, *Mandate to Difference*, 60.

nation into an immense and inclusive gathering for worship. This is the God who teaches us and judges us fairly, not arbitrarily; the God of peace, not the God of war and violence. This is the God who seeks the well-being of all and who would remove from all the fears that beset us.

While Isaiah 2 and Micah 4 bear witness to a hospitable God, they implicitly challenge us to imagine a world very different from the one we actually experience. They invite us to imagine a world where a gracious God is in charge, where people from every nation gather for worship, where people seek God's instruction, a disarmed world of peace without violence or fear. Could it be that this vision's witness to a hospitable God and its implied challenge to imagine a different kind of world are its purposes? Could it be that *we*, along with the faithful in every generation, are this vision's intended recipients? These are certainly possibilities.

The Holy Spirit and Vision

Joel 2:28–32a and Acts 2:17–21 are two versions of the same prophetic oracle. The versions appear in different contexts. Their introductory phrases are different; and two adjectives, "terrible" and "glorious," that describe "the day of the Lord" in Joel 2:31 and Acts 2:20 are the opposite of each other. Otherwise the two versions are almost identical, and the Acts 2 version clearly acknowledges that Joel's version is the original of the two.[20]

The book of Joel opens with a lament over the devastation that locusts have inflicted upon the land's crops and livestock.[21] A call for repentance and prayer[22] and a promise of God's mercy follow.[23] Then the book introduces our prophetic oracle with the phrase that the NRSV translates "Then afterward." This phrase denotes transition from God's judgment to God's redemption, and it

---

20. Acts 2:16.
21. Joel 1:2–12.
22. Joel 1:13—2:17
23. Joel 2:18–27.

introduces us to the relationship between the spirit and vision. In the oracle God speaks:

> I will pour out my spirit on all flesh;
> your sons and your daughters shall prophesy,
>> your old men shall dream dreams,
>> and your young men shall see visions.
> Even on the male and female slaves,
>> in those days, I will pour out my spirit.
>
> I will show portents in the heaven and on the earth. . . . The sun shall be turned to darkness, and the moon to blood, before the great and terrible day of the Lord comes. Then everyone who calls on the name of the Lord shall be saved.[24]

The Spirit of God is to be poured out and made available to all, female and male, old and young, the free and the enslaved. Furthermore, the gifts of the Spirit will be available to all: prophecy, dreams, and visions. Even when God shows portents in heaven and on earth, even when the sun is darkened and the moon bloodied, even when the "terrible day" comes, salvation is available to all. Prophecy, dreams, visions, and salvation itself are gifts from God and available to all through God's Spirit.

But in Acts 2 the prophetic oracle appears in an altogether different context. Instead of locusts and calls for repentance and prayer, the day of Pentecost has come. The sound of rushing wind filled the house, and each person in the crowd heard others speak in their own "native language." Many were "amazed and perplexed," while others "sneered" and accused the crowd of public drunkenness.[25] At this point Peter addressed the crowd. He noted how absurd the charge of drunkenness was when he said, "For it is only nine o'clock in the morning."[26] Then he reached back to the Old Testament, specifically to the prophet Joel; and Joel's prophetic oracle became a sermon text for Pentecost.

24. Joel 2:28–32a.
25. Acts 2:6, 12, 13.
26. Acts 2:15.

According to Acts 2, Peter's reading of Joel's oracle gave the oracle a new introduction. Instead of transition from judgment to redemption, the new introduction begins, "In the last days it will be, says God."[27] This introduction signifies, according to Paul Feine and Johannes Behm, "the beginning of the eschatological time of salvation."[28] Nevertheless, except for this change in the introductory phrase and the change in the description of the "day of the Lord," the text that Peter reportedly read was almost identical to Joel's original oracle. Using the prophet's own words, Peter declared that Joel had foretold the coming of the Spirit in and through events similar to those the crowd had just seen and experienced; and that Joel had identified prophecy, visions, and dreams as gifts of the Spirit available to all, to women and men, old and young, slave and free. Furthermore Peter, through Joel's oracle, declared that salvation is available to everyone who calls on the name of the Lord.

Both Joel 2 and Acts 2 affirm that the coming of the Spirit releases prophecy, visions, and dreams into the world. Moreover, the line "Your young men shall see visions"[29] is the first mention of vision in the book of Acts. This line, with its connection to the coming of the Spirit, is the background to and sets the tone for all the vision stories in Acts.

Luke's Texts about Seeing

Although Acts 2:17 is the first mention of vision in the book of Acts, it is not the first indication of interest in vision in the Luke-Acts corpus. Three texts in Luke, 12:54–56; 18:35–43; and 19:1–10, are about aspects of seeing. The first text is one of Jesus' teachings. The second is the story of Jesus' healing a blind beggar, and the third is the story of Jesus and Zacchaeus. None of these texts specifically mention vision, but all of them complement our understanding of vision and visioning.

---

27. Acts 2:17.
28. Feine and Behm, *Introduction to the New Testament*, 121.
29. Acts 2:17.

Expanding Perspectives: More Texts about Vision

According to Luke 12:54, Jesus spoke "to the crowds." Here is my translation of Luke's text of Jesus' words in verses 54–56:

> When you see a cloud rising in the west, you say at once that a rainstorm is coming; and so it happens. And when a south wind is blowing, you say that there will be a burning heat; and it happens. Hypocrites, you know to examine the appearance of the earth and the heaven. So, why do you not examine the present time?[30]

Jesus opened his teaching by citing weather patterns observable in Eastern Mediterranean countries: "When you see a cloud rising in the west," and, "When a south wind is blowing." Next he identified the conclusions drawn from each observation: "you say at once that a rainstorm is coming," and, "you say that there will be a burning heat." He then confirmed the accuracy of both conclusions with the phrase "and it happens."

In 12:56a Jesus shifted from seeing to knowing, from specific observations to the process of obtaining knowledge from these observations. "You know to examine the appearance of the earth and the heaven," he said. The verb that I have translated "examine" means "test, try, examine, prove." It appears in a variety of New Testament texts: "*Examine* yourselves, and only then eat of the bread and drink of the cup."[31] "I *am testing* the genuineness of your love against the earnestness of others."[32] "Beloved, do not believe every spirit, but *test* the spirits to see whether they are from God."[33] The italicized words are translations of the same verb that I translated with "examine" in Luke 12:56. This verb probably originated in ancient metallurgy, where it meant "assay." To assay is to test or analyze a compound (such as an ore) for the presence of a specific substance or metal, often by burning or heating the compound. The color of the flame as the compound burned or the residue left after the compound cooled were often signs of the presence

---

30. Cf. Matt 16:2–3.
31. 1 Cor 11:28.
32. 2 Cor 8:8.
33. 1 John 4:1.

or absence of the substance desired. First Peter 1:7 describes the assay process and uses the verb meaning "test" or "examine" when it speaks of faith as "being more precious than gold that, though perishable, *is tested* by fire."[34]

But how should we interpret Jesus' question in 12:56b: "Why do you not examine the present time?" Gunther Bornkamm interpreted it as follows:

> We understand now Jesus' sharp word against foolish speculation, which tries to reckon the beginning of the kingdom of God from cosmic signs, as the farmer tries to forecast the rain from the rising cloud and the heat of the next day from the south wind (Lk. xii.54ff). This is more than a condemnation of the boldness which ventures with an air of wisdom to deal with questions surpassing the powers of man. . . . He who looks forth to find the kingdom of God as he would look at the weather or any other event which can be observed . . . not only wants to know too much, but is fundamentally in error about God and himself.[35]

And Bornkamm added that examining the present time means "to lay hold on the hour of salvation."[36]

I agree with Bornkamm's interpretation of the phrase "examine the present time." However, I would interpret Jesus' question differently. Jesus did not ask, "Why do you examine the present time?" If he had, I would agree wholeheartedly with Bornkamm's interpretation. Jesus asked instead, "Why do you *not* examine the present time?" Jesus wasn't challenging his hearers' "foolish speculation," "airs of wisdom" about questions beyond human knowledge, or their wanting "to know too much." Instead he was challenging their hypocrisy in their failure to look at and to examine what God was doing in and through Jesus' presence and

---

34. I am indebted to the late Dr. Stuart D. Currie, who, in the early 1960s, taught me and my fellow classmates about the Greek word for "test" or "examine" and about the importance of the Greek New Testament's vocabulary. Dr. Currie died suddenly in 1975.

35. Bornkamm, *Jesus of Nazareth*, 74–75.

36. Ibid., 87.

Expanding Perspectives: More Texts about Vision

ministry. You have the ability to see weather-related phenomena and to forecast accordingly, he argued. So, why don't you use that ability to look at "the present time" of God's presence and salvation in the world? Why do you not see and examine the Messiah who is already in your midst?

When we turn from Luke 12:54–56 to 18:35–43 and 19:1–10, we are turning from a failure to see to two desires to see. The types of seeing desired, however, are quite different in the two stories. The first story begins with Jesus on the road to Jericho and a blind man begging by the roadside. When the blind man heard a crowd on the road, he asked what was happening. The crowd told him, "Jesus of Nazareth is passing by."[37] Upon hearing that Jesus was nearby, the blind man shouted, "Jesus, Son of David, have mercy upon me!"[38] His shout was a plea for help, a plea that presupposed a belief in the ability of Jesus to help; and when members of the crowd sternly ordered him to be quiet, he repeated his plea even more loudly than before. Jesus, no doubt hearing the shouts, stopped and ordered someone to bring the blind man to him, gestures that apparently calmed the commotion. Jesus then asked the blind man, "What do you want me to do for you?" and the man replied, "Lord, let me see again."[39] The blind man wanted his physical sight restored. His desire was to "see again."

The blind man got what he wanted. His belief in the ability of Jesus to help was correct. Jesus said to him, "Receive your sight; your faith has saved you."[40] He regained his sight immediately, and both he and those who witnessed his healing praised God for Jesus' work of restoring his sight.

After the healing of the blind beggar, Jesus entered Jericho; and the opening sentences of 19:1–10 introduce us to Zacchaeus, a Jericho resident, and the story of his encounter with Jesus. Zacchaeus "was a chief tax collector and was rich."[41] Tax collectors

37. Luke 18:37.
38. Luke 18:38.
39. Luke 18:41.
40. Luke 18:42.
41. Luke 19:2.

in first-century Palestine were often Jews whom the Romans employed to collect taxes and customs duties that the Romans had levied. Because of their close association with Roman authorities, many Jews believed tax collectors to be "sinners," even traitors to the Jewish faith. And because collecting taxes for the Romans was quite lucrative, many Jews believed tax collectors to be corrupt, a charge likely to have been true in many cases. Zacchaeus, however, wasn't an average tax collector. He was a *chief* tax collector, with all of the wealth and low social and religious esteem that would have accompanied his job. Furthermore, "he was trying to see who Jesus was"; but he couldn't see over the crowd "because he was short in stature."[42] So, to ensure himself a glimpse of Jesus when he passed by, Zacchaeus ran ahead of the crowd and climbed a tree.

Zacchaeus also got what he wanted, and more. Jesus called to him, "Zacchaeus, come down."[43] Jesus visited him, "I must stay at your house today," and Zacchaeus gladly welcomed him.[44] But the people of Jericho reacted to Jesus associating with a tax collector and grumbled, "He has gone to be the guest of . . . a sinner."[45] Meanwhile Zacchaeus offered Jesus his confession and repentance, "Half of my possessions, Lord, I will give to the poor; and if I have defrauded anyone of anything, I will pay back four times as much."[46] Jesus' response to Zacchaeus' repentance was threefold. (1) Jesus declared, "Today salvation has come to this house."[47] (2) He challenged the stereotypical Jewish view of tax collectors as sinners and corrupt: "He too is a son of Abraham."[48] (3) And he reiterated his mission in the world: "For the Son of Man came to seek out and to save the lost."[49] As Bornkamm said, "[Jesus] is often ready and on the spot sooner than the sufferers dare hope, and he

42. Luke 19:3.
43. Luke 19:5.
44. Luke 19:5–6.
45. Luke 19:7.
46. Luke 19:8.
47. Luke 19:9.
48. Luke 19:9.
49. Luke 19:10.

freely breaks through the strict boundaries which traditions and prejudices had set up."[50] Zacchaeus experienced for himself Jesus' boundary-breaking ministry.

Although not obvious from the beginning, Luke's three texts about seeing share a common subject: Jesus the Messiah. The text in Luke 12 is about a failure to see God at work in Jesus. The text in Luke 18 is about a blind man's desire that Jesus restore his sight, and the Luke 19 text is about a "sinner's" desire to see who Jesus was. Whether about a failure to see or a desire to see, all three texts point us to the person who was and is our ultimate vision of God in and for our world.

Where There Is No Vision: Proverbs 29:18

"Where is Proverbs 29:18? Surely you've studied it and thought about it. Why didn't you write about it?" asked a prepublication reviewer of my work.

"Because people treat it too cavalierly," I replied.

"Then say that!" she said.[51]

My reviewer's challenge startled me, but her challenge was on target. Yes, I had studied carefully Proverbs 29:18. Yes, I had thought seriously about its meaning. My reviewer was right when she challenged me to put in writing what I had learned and was thinking, to speak out without hesitation about a well-known biblical text on vision.

But my reply to my reviewer's challenge deserves a hearing, for I did not reply flippantly or thoughtlessly. On far too many occasions, I had seen the King James Version of Proverbs 29:18 ("Where there is no vision, the people perish.") cited as a rationale for participation in a visioning process. I knew from my study that Proverbs 29:18 is deeper and richer in meaning than any one-line rationale for a management process, and I knew from personal experience that church members and leaders were weary of overly

---

50. Bornkamm, *Jesus of Nazareth*, 59.
51. A conversation with Dr. Cynthia Rigby on April 9, 2015.

simple and cliché-filled interpretations of this proverb. So, in what ways do people treat this proverb too cavalierly? In my experience this happens when readers or interpreters ignore or neglect one or more of the following: (1) the context of Proverbs 29:18, (2) the poetic structure of this proverb, or (3) the meanings of this proverb's vocabulary.

Proverbs 29:18 does not stand alone in the book of Proverbs. It is not a miscellaneous proverb in the midst of other miscellaneous proverbs, as are the proverbs in Proverbs 10–22:16. It is instead one proverb in a collection of proverbs in Proverbs 28–29, a collection of proverbs with common themes and chosen by sages to serve a common purpose. Authority, government, the use and abuse of power, leadership, economic justice or injustice, and a variety of related moral questions are common themes in this collection, as the following proverbs illustrate:

> Like a roaring lion or a charging bear
> is a wicked ruler over poor people.
> A ruler who lacks understanding is a cruel oppressor;
> but one who hates unjust gain will enjoy a long life.
>
> When the righteous are in authority, the people rejoice;
> but when the wicked rule, the people groan.
>
> By justice a king gives stability to the land,
> but one who makes heavy exactions ruins it.
>
> If a ruler listens to falsehood,
> all his officials will be wicked.
>
> Many seek the favor of a ruler,
> but it is from the Lord that one gets justice.[52]

These and other proverbs, including 29:18, appear to have been collected to instruct up-and-coming leaders in the art of good government and the proper exercise of authority.

Christine Roy Yoder, as part of a study on Proverbs 30, summarized the effects of Proverbs 28–29 on its intended readers:

---

52. Prov 28:15, 16; Prov 29:2, 4, 12, 26

Expanding Perspectives: More Texts about Vision

At the close of Prov. 28–29, readers are poised for the invitation to "come up here" (Prov. 25:7) and assume a position of leadership. Schooled further by court scribes and adept with more proverbs of Solomon, they are nuanced in their thinking about the possibilities and perils of authority and government, and alert to a moral arena defined largely in terms of "[the] people[s]," rich and poor, wicked and righteous, wise and foolish. Presumably, they are also optimistic about the accessibility of wisdom and their capacity to interpret the world and navigate its complexities intelligently.[53]

Yoder's summary also serves as a description of the context in which 29:18 appears.

But if Proverbs 29:18 does not stand alone in the book of Proverbs, the statement on vision in 29:18 also does not stand alone within the proverb itself. Scholars have long known that lines of Hebrew poetry typically combine two statements in such a way that the statements are "parallel" to each other, in that they are variations on the same idea. "This may come about by the second [statement] repeating the content of the first in different words (synonymous parallelism), or it may be that it sets it off sharply with a contrasting thought (antithetic parallelism), or it may be that it simply takes the thought further and completes it (synthetic parallelism)."[54]

Like the vast majority of proverbs in the book of Proverbs, 29:18 is one line of Hebrew poetry. And like the majority of proverbs in Proverbs 28–29, it combines two contrasting statements; its parallelism is antithetical. Such parallelism suggests that we consider both statements simultaneously and in relation to each other. We cannot interpret the first statement about vision without also interpreting the second statement about *torah*, and vice versa. Proverbs 29:18 speaks to up-and-coming leaders about both vision and *torah*.

When we turn to this proverb's vocabulary, we soon encounter the noun usually translated, "vision." This noun is derived from a verb whose meaning is usually restricted to "seeing a vision" from

---

53. Yoder, "On the Threshold of Kingship," 259.
54. Eissfeldt, *Old Testament*, 57.

God or "seeing a revelation."[55] Therefore, "vision" or "revelation" are probably the best translations of this noun. Some scholars, based on the observations that this noun appears in 29:18 in parallel to *torah* and that it appears in the opening sentences of Isaiah and Nahum, have translated this noun with the word "prophecy." This is certainly a possible translation. However, nothing in Proverbs 28–29 or in 29:18 by itself requires this translation; and there are other Hebrew words that clearly mean, "prophesy, prophet, or prophecy." I will stand by the translation "vision," based on the restricted meaning of its root verb, "see a vision."

The NRSV translates the main clause of the first statement in 29:18, "The people cast off restraint." This is an appropriate translation. The Hebrew verb in this clause is a passive form of a verb that means "loosen." In its passive form it means "be let loose," "lack restraint," or "lack self-control."[56] This verb does not mean "perish," as the King James Version translates it. Vision is not a matter of life vs. death. It is instead a matter of clarity vs. confusion or chaos; focus vs. fuzziness; self-discipline and self-control, both personally and communally, vs. a loss of discipline and control.

The second statement in 29:18 opens with a participle form of a verb meaning "keep, guard, or observe" followed by the noun *torah*. This statement means "Those keeping *torah*" or "Those who keep *torah*." *Torah* is often, sometimes appropriately, translated with the word "law." But, as one of my Jewish friends has repeatedly reminded me, *torah* is not necessarily law or regulation. It is frequently "teaching" or "instruction." And the five books of the *Torah* are not exclusively law codes. They include stories of God's creation, of the family and descendants of Abraham, of slavery and the exodus from Egypt, of wilderness wandering, and of the gift of ten "words" of God at Mount Sinai—i.e., stories of God's gracious actions in history. These five books teach us to love God, neighbors, and strangers and to treat the land and people around us with justice and mercy. When Proverbs 29:18 speaks of those who keep *torah*, it is referring to those who keep God's teaching,

---

55. Jepsen, "chazah," 290.
56. Brown et al., *Hebrew and English Lexicon*, 829.

God's instruction. And when it draws the parallel between vision and *torah*, it is telling us that God's teaching, God's instruction, informs and undergirds our vision; or at least it ought to.

Proverbs 29:18 ends with a word meaning "blessed" or "happy." "Happy" has a modern ring to it; but it also sounds more flippant than serious, more like a popular self-help book than a proverb for guiding an up-and-coming leader. "Blessed" may sound a bit old fashioned, but at least it alludes to God and God's gifts of vision and *torah* on which faithful leaders will depend.

To leaders, both ancient and modern, I offer my translation of Proverbs 29:18:

> Where there is no vision, the people lose self-control,
> but those who keep [God's] instruction are blessed.

About vision in particular, this proverb says: When there is no vision that is informed and undergirded by God's teaching, we should expect confusion and chaos, a lack of focus, and a loss of self-discipline and self-control, both personally and communally.

6

Toward Understanding Vision

A VISION IS A mode or form of seeing an object(s), scene(s), event(s), or person(s).[1] Although dictionary definitions of vision can be divided into two categories, those that define vision as an act of seeing or causing to see and those that define it as the sight or thing seen, vision consists of both an act of seeing or causing to see and the sight or thing seen.[2] Without the act of seeing or causing to see, no sight or thing can be seen; and without the sight or thing seen, no act of seeing or causing to see will have occurred. Definitions of vision that reduce it either to an act or to something seen are inevitably incomplete.[3]

In the course of healthy human experience, there are three primary modes or forms of seeing; and thus, there are three types of vision. Although additional modes of seeing are theoretically possible, other potential modes, when examined carefully, almost always prove to be variants of one of the three primary forms. This chapter will examine each of the three modes or forms of seeing, their interrelationships, and theological issues surrounding them.

1. Cf. Wolin, *Politics and Vision*, 17–18.

2. *Random House Dictionary*, 1597; *Webster's Ninth New Collegiate Dictionary*, 1318; *Webster's Third New International Dictionary*, 2557.

3. For a discussion of the philosophical connection between the various functions of the imagination, of which visual imagination is one, and the imagination's image-making function, see Warnock, *Imagination*, 172–73, 183, 190, 192–95.

The chapter will conclude with comments on a biblical story that illustrates, either explicitly or indirectly, the three forms of seeing and with some practical suggestions for understanding and using three types of vision.

This chapter will not cover chemically induced modes of seeing or visions and hallucinations that are sometimes the symptoms of illnesses or other pathological disorders. Such topics belong to medical research and practice and are far beyond the scope of this chapter and the understanding of this writer.

Physical Seeing

Except for those who were born blind or who lost their eyesight at a very young age, physical seeing was and is our first form of seeing. At an early age we saw objects and scenes, people and events; and most of us have continued to see with our eyes even though our sight may have grown weaker with the passing years.

We can say that physical seeing was and is our first form of seeing in two respects. First, it was the chronological beginning of our seeing, the starting point of our visual experience of people and events, scenes and objects around us. It was the inception of our visual perceptions, those visual impressions, understandings, or images that we hold in our memories and constantly refine and rethink through our human experiences.

Second, physical seeing was and is our first form of seeing in that we consider it the basis, the paradigm, the pattern for all our seeing. As we have matured, we have experienced other forms of seeing; but we still refer to our first form. Physical seeing is the guiding paradigm by which we understand and interpret other forms of seeing. Our use of the phrase "I see" to indicate our understanding attests to the paradigmatic power of physical seeing.

Physical seeing is sensory. It is one of the human body's five senses along with hearing, touch, taste, and smell. We can describe it physiologically. It involves the eyes and the brain. Here is a brief physiological description of physical sight:

> Light from a visual stimulus is inverted as it passes through the lens. It then hits the retina at the back of the eye, where light-sensitive cells turn it into a message of electrical pulses. These are carried along the optic nerve from each eye and cross over at the optic chiasma—a major anatomical landmark. The optic track then carries the information to the lateral geniculate body, part of the thalamus. This shunts it on to [the visual cortex] at the back of the brain. The visual cortex is split into many areas, each processing an aspect of sight, such as colour, shape, size and so on.[4]

The crossover of electrical pulses at the optic chiasma ensures that optic messages travel through both of the brain's hemispheres. The thalamus is part of the inner brain's limbic system, the system that generates our emotions. Thanks to the thalamus, things seen are sometimes emotion laden. And different areas of the visual cortex are the brain's way of handling the complexity of visual stimuli. Our physical seeing takes only nanoseconds. Even to those of us who must wear eyeglasses, our first type of vision feels instantaneous and effortless.

Physical seeing, sensory vision, makes a range of human experiences possible. Through it we witness all sorts of human behavior and human emotions. We see love and affection among parents and children, spouses and friends. We observe brutality, violence, and hate among neighbors, nations, and sometimes fellow workers. We notice laughter, joy, and pleasant surprises among families and in social gatherings. We recognize sorrow, disappointment, fear, and anger in the surrounding world. Through sensory vision we enjoy all sorts of aesthetic beauty: the natural world with its diversity of color, size, and purpose; the human body with its shape, form, and allure; the creations of artists, from the artwork of children magnetically attached to refrigerator doors to the paintings of masters in the world's greatest galleries. Through physical seeing we make scientific and historical observations: telescopically viewing stars and planets, microscopically studying cells and

---

4. Carter, *Mapping the Mind*, 112.

Toward Understanding Vision

viruses, and carefully watching the events and trends of the day for signs of an unfolding future. Through sensory vision human communication is facilitated as we notice gestures, bodily movements, and facial expressions. So broad is the range of human experience made possible through physical seeing that we dare not underestimate or take for granted this form of vision.

Physical seeing, however, is limited in its time perspective. It only sees the visual stimuli available in the present moment. It cannot see either the past or the future. In the present it can, of course, observe the evidence of the past: documents, letters, photographs, artifacts, and so on. In the present it can watch someone tell stories from the past: family stories, national stories, faith stories; but it can never re-create exactly the events, people, objects, or scenes that once existed. Likewise, it cannot create or foretell the future. It can observe projections, plans, goals, and other presently visible signs of some possible future. It can recognize dreams, hopes, or fears that people currently express about the future; but it cannot see precisely what lies ahead. Although it makes possible a range of human experiences, this type of vision sees only a physical now.

Physical seeing is part of God's creation. God brought into being all things and all creatures, including humankind and all of humankind's attributes. Genesis 1 attests to God's creation of humankind and to the goodness of God's whole creation:

> Then God said, "Let us make humankind in our image, according to our likeness." . . . So God created humankind in his image. . . . God saw everything that he had made, and indeed, it was very good.[5]

Psalm 8 praises God for God's work of creating human beings and for giving humans a place of honor and responsibility among the orders of creation:

> When I look at your heavens, the work of your fingers,
> The moon and the stars that you have established;
> What are human beings that you are mindful of them,
> Mortals that you care for them?

5. Gen 1:26–27, 31.

> Yet you have made them a little lower than God,
> And crowned them with glory and honor.
> You have given them dominion over the works of your hands;
> You have put all things under their feet.[6]

And Psalm 94:9 specifically mentions God's formation of our eyesight:

> He who planted the ear, does he not hear?
> He who formed the eye, does he not see?

Like much of creation, physical sight is a sign of God's love for and kindness toward all human beings. When Jesus in the Sermon on the Mount taught disciples to replace the conventional wisdom of loving neighbors and hating enemies with a radical ethic of also loving one's enemies, he predicated his teaching on this rationale: "For [God] makes his sun rise on the evil and on the good, and sends rain on the righteous and on the unrighteous."[7] Jesus perceived that two ordinary natural phenomena, sunshine and rainfall, are signs of God's graciousness poured out upon all, even upon the undeserving. Jesus could easily have used two of the five senses, vision and hearing, to make the same point. When Paul compared the church to a human body with its many members, he frequently mentioned eyes and hearing:

> If the ear would say, "Because I am not an eye, I do not belong to the body," that would not make it any less a part of the body. If the whole body were an eye, where would the hearing be? If the whole body were hearing, where would the sense of smell be? . . . The eye cannot say to the hand, "I have no need of you."[8]

Paul clearly understood the important roles of vision and hearing in human functioning. And Jesus in the Sermon on the Mount says with respect to eyesight, "The eye is the lamp of the body. So,

---

6. Ps 8:3–6.
7. Matt 5:45.
8. 1 Cor 12:16–17, 21a.

if your eye is healthy, your whole body will be full of light."[9] First Corinthians and the Sermon on the Mount both imply that physical seeing is indeed a sign of God's grace.

But physical seeing, because human will and error often direct its use, is also fallible and sinful. Jeremiah acknowledged its fallibility when he wrote:

> Hear this, O foolish and senseless people,
> > who have eyes, but do not see,
> > who have ears, but do not hear.[10]

The book of Job provides a vivid illustration of the eye's participation in sin:

> The murderer rises at dusk
> > to kill the poor and needy,
> > and in the night is like a thief.
> The eye of the adulterer also waits for the twilight,
> > saying, "No eye will see me";
> > and he disguises his face.[11]

And immediately after Jesus in the Sermon on the Mount identifies the eye as "the lamp of the body" and describes a healthy eye as the source of the body's light, he says, "But if your eye is unhealthy, your whole body will be full of darkness."[12] So, is physical seeing healthy or unhealthy, full of light or full of darkness? Is it God's grace or human weakness and imperfection? In fact, it is both. This is how it is with all creation and all its parts, even its marvelous parts like physical sight. This type of vision, like the rest of creation, lives in the tension between pointing to God's goodness and participating in human error.

---

9. Matt 6:22.
10. Jer 5:21.
11. Job 24:14–15.
12. Matt 6:23a.

Mental Seeing

The second mode or form of seeing, and thus the second type of vision, is mental seeing. This form of seeing differs physiologically from physical sight in two respects. First, it is extrasensory. It involves the human brain, but does not involve eyesight or any of the other senses. In mental seeing the act of seeing and the image(s) seen occur entirely within the brain and its complex web of neural connections to the rest of the human body.

Second, the brain's activity in mental seeing begins more or less when and where its activity in physical seeing ends. After the visual cortex receives and processes information derived from visual stimuli, the brain's frontal cortex coordinates and directs the information to various areas throughout the brain depending on the nature of the information. Sometimes it sends the information to an area of the brain to be acted upon immediately. Sometimes it stores the information as perception in the memory, and sometimes it combines the information with other information and sends both to another area of the frontal cortex where they may be used to conceive or devise concepts.

It is important to note at this point that the brains of healthy adults and many adolescents are able to retrieve, reuse, reconceive, and restore information in their memories and that they are able to recombine and reconsider information to create new images, sounds, or concepts. Our brains are constantly reusing and recombining information, as well as receiving new information through the senses. Out of the interplay of these processes, mental seeing takes place; and mental visions are engendered.

Current neuroscience maintains, "The memory capacity of a human brain is effectively infinite, providing it is stored in the right way."[13] It also contends "that there is no rigid dividing line between a memory and a thought. A new term has therefore crept into use to describe how we juggle perceptions, memories and concepts: working memory."[14] When we visualize or imagine a solution to a

---

13. Carter, *Mapping the Mind*, 175.
14. Ibid., 188.

complex problem or a new way of illustrating or doing something, we are in fact "juggling perceptions, memories and concepts"; and out of this juggling our mental seeing may become visualized or imaginative.

The word "imaginative" brings us to the subject of vision as imagination. What is the relationship between mental vision and imagination? Are they synonymous?

Interlude on Imagination

In a 1929 interview published in *The Saturday Evening Post*, Albert Einstein remarked, "Imagination is more important than knowledge. Knowledge is limited. Imagination encircles the world."[15] Einstein's remark not only highlights imagination's importance, it also calls attention to its breadth, to its ability to look beyond the boundaries of knowledge. But although imagination is important, it is also a complex subject, much too complex for a thorough treatment in this brief chapter. Nevertheless, if we intend to understand the similarity and dissimilarity between mental vision and imagination, we need some basic information about imagination. Four statements about imagination might facilitate our understanding.

1. *A thorough study of imagination requires a multidisciplinary approach.* At a minimum, such a study involves the disciplines of neuroscience, philosophy, psychology, aesthetics, literature, and a variety of the visual arts. To this list we could add a host of ancillary subjects in the natural sciences, the social sciences, and the arts. And if we are considering religious imagination or imagination in relationship to God or aspects of theology, then we must add to the list hermeneutics (the principles of interpretation) and a variety of theological subjects.

Even if we limit our study of imagination to one discipline, it will still be complicated. The study of imagination in philosophy, for example, is in itself complex. Philosopher Mary Warnock traced the concept of imagination from David Hume's 1739 *Treatise of Human*

---

15. Viereck, "What Life Means to Einstein," 117.

Old Man Dreaming

Nature to the early 1970s.[16] Along the way she analyzed the thinking of Hume, Kant, Schelling, Coleridge, Wordsworth, Ryle, Wittgenstein, Sartre, and others. Each philosopher and writer used his own language, definitions, illustrations, and arguments; and Coleridge and Wordsworth sometimes expressed their ideas in their poetry. Merely to trace the concept of imagination, Warnock had to clarify and assess the theories and counter-theories, the arguments and counter-arguments, of each philosopher and writer.

As she traced the concept of imagination, Warnock reconsidered her own views about imagination. Early in her study, she recognized the importance of Immanuel Kant's ideas on imagination. Based on those ideas, Warnock argued that "it is the representational power of the imagination, its power . . . actually to form images, ideas or likenesses in the mind which is supposed to contribute to our awareness of the world."[17] Following Kant's lead, philosophers tried to understand imagination through understanding images. By the early twentieth century, however, it was clear that the imagination served more functions than making images. Wrote Warnock, "In order to understand the image, we need to understand the diverse but related functions of imagination."[18] But how is it possible to connect and understand functions as diverse as making mental pictures, creating works of art, interpreting what we see, and forming meaningful symbols? Warnock answered by referring to Wittgenstein's concepts of "seeing as" or "noticing an aspect" and to his linking of these concepts with "having an image."[19] Warnock concluded:

> The connection between seeing an aspect of something and having an image . . . is clear. . . . [W]e cannot separate the interpretative function of the imagination from its image-forming function. . . . Imagination is our means of

---

16. Warnock, *Imagination*.
17. Ibid., 33.
18. Ibid., 172–73.
19. Ibid., 183, 190, 192–93.

interpreting the world, and it is also our means of forming images in the mind.[20]

Warnock had revised her understanding of imagination from adherence to Kant's views to a more complex understanding via Wittgenstein's thought.

2. *There are other forms of imagination besides the visual.*[21] For example, there is sound or auditory imagination. Musical composition, song writing, and some poetry are evidence of this form of imagination. There is also conceptual imagination. Aspects of mathematics, public policy formation, organizational planning, and formation of scientific hypotheses and theories rely on this form of imagination. And additional forms of imagination are possible.

A list of every form of imagination is not important at this point. What is important is the recognition that imagination is larger than and encompasses more than mental seeing. Imagination and mental seeing are not synonymous. Imagination is the more comprehensive of the two. Nevertheless, *visual* imagination and mental seeing are very similar. In fact, they are similar enough that we can probably consider the phrases "visual imagination" and "mental vision" to be virtually synonymous (provided we continue to modify the word "imagination" with the word "visual").

3. *Imagination is now a major category in theological studies.* In fact, it's so pervasive a category that listing and commenting on all the scholars and theologians who have developed or used concepts related to imagination would require a rather long paper or book. I will mention and comment on three such scholars and theologians.

New Testament scholar Amos Wilder was one of the earlier writers on imagination in theology. In the opening pages of his 1976 book *Theopoetic*, he wrote:

> It is at the level of the imagination that the fateful issues of our new world-experience must first be mastered. It

20. Ibid., 194–95.

21. For a discussion of ocular metaphors and their problems, see Bryant, *Faith and the Play of Imagination*, 103–5.

is here that culture and history are broken, and here that the church is polarized.²²

We should recognize that human nature and human societies are more deeply motivated by images and fabulations than by ideas. This is where power lies and the future is shaped. . . . Imagination is a necessary component of all profound knowing and celebration; all remembering, realizing, and anticipating; all faith, hope, and love. When imagination fails doctrines become ossified, witness and proclamation wooden, doxologies and litanies empty, consolations hollow, and ethics legalistic.²³

Wilder's focus on imagination was by no means frivolous or based on fantasy. On the contrary, he argued that our explorations into the imagination "should be carried out in dialogue with the insights and accumulated wisdom of our older religious traditions."²⁴ Alluding to 1 Thessalonians 5:19–21 and 1 John 4:1, he advised, "The Spirit is not to be quenched, yet the spirits should be tested."²⁵ And he understood the necessity of balancing imagination and tradition when he wrote:

> Any plea for a valid theopoetic today must defend itself on two fronts. It must assert the rights of the imagination against abstraction, rationalism, and stereotype. But the enemy is also on the other side: the cult of the imagination for itself alone; vision, phantasy, ecstasy for their own sakes; creativity, spontaneity on their own, without roots, without tradition, without discipline.²⁶

Wilder's emphasis on imagination's communal contexts is noteworthy. In the opening lines of *Theopoetic*, we read about "our new world-experience," "culture and history . . . broken," and "church . . . polarized"; and in the line cited in the previous paragraph, we read about "creativity . . . without roots, without

22. Wilder, *Theopoetic*, 1.
23. Ibid., 2.
24. Ibid., 16.
25. Ibid., 22.
26. Ibid., 57.

tradition, without discipline." These are clearly references to communal contexts. Wilder obviously intended that imagination be exercised and tested in community, either in the community of humankind or in the community of the faithful.

In the preface to *An Introduction to the Old Testament*, Walter Brueggemann referred to Amos Wilder as one of "two giants in the field of interpretation."[27] Early on in the same work, he also outlined his concept "imaginative remembering." Remembering, said Brueggemann, took place in the formation of the Bible and takes place today in the faith community when one generation tells and retells the faith stories to children and grandchildren. In this telling and retelling there was and is an interplay of history and theological intentionality, an imaginative interplay designed both to communicate the community's faith and history and to make faith a lively possibility for younger generations. The process of this interplay is the work of tradition and may be called "imaginative remembering."[28]

Brueggemann argued that the traditioning process that formed the church's Scripture "is not an innocent act of reportage," but "an intentional advocacy that means to tilt the world of the next generation" toward faith.[29] He identified facets of this process, one of which is Scripture as a "relentless act of imagination" in that it imagines "a world defined by the character of YHWH."[30]

Brueggemann warned that imagination could be used idolatrously.[31] Nevertheless, he continued to advocate for imagination's place in Scripture's formation and in the church's interpretation of it:

> It is through the work of faithful imagination that the text of Scripture has been produced. In a quite similar way, it is clear that interpretation of Scripture . . . continues in faithful church practices to be an act of imagination that

---

27. Brueggemann, *Introduction to the Old Testament*, xiii.
28. Ibid., 7–9.
29. Ibid., 9.
30. Ibid., 9–10.
31. Ibid., 13.

is congruent with the imaginative character of the text itself.³²

Those familiar with Brueggemann's works know that his own interpretations of Scripture texts are deeply imaginative and sensitive to human and ecclesiastical communities.

Like Brueggemann, David J. Bryant also referred to Amos Wilder at the beginning of his book *Faith and the Play of Imagination*.³³ Bryant's subject, however, was not biblical interpretation, but imagination itself. Drawing on the work of philosophers Kant, Warnock, Ricoeur, and Gadamer, Bryant agreed with theologian Gordon Kaufman that "faith and theology are thoroughly imaginative"; but he disagreed with Kaufman's view that imagination is only a "constructive activity."³⁴ He argued instead for replacing Kaufman's view with "an understanding of the imagination that places it solidly in the historical nature of human life and thereby regards it as both constructive and receptive."³⁵ In arguing his case, Bryant broadened and modified Warnock's concept of imagination to include the power of "taking as" as well as the power of "seeing as." "I prefer," wrote Bryant, "to define imagination as the power of 'taking as,' underscoring the element of individual and communal praxis in imagination."³⁶

With a receptive imagination defined as "taking as," imagination is open to traditions, including biblical and Christian faith traditions, and their interplay among experiences, feelings, and constructed concepts. For Christians, wrote Bryant, "The imagination attunes us to what is disclosed through faith's traditions. A tradition's disclosive power, then, is what shapes the imagination

---

32. Ibid., 396.
33. Bryant, *Faith and the Play of Imagination*, 1.
34. Ibid., 64, 201.
35. Ibid., 202–3.
36. Ibid., 205.

and gives rise to faith."[37] Bryant added, "The work of theology depends on the prior imaginative construal of faith."[38]

4. *The Presbyterian Church (U.S.A.)'s eighth ordination question exemplifies imagination's appropriate place in the faith and practice of Christian communities.*[39] Readers who are not Presbyterians will understandably ask for an explanation at this point.

All candidates for ordination in the Presbyterian Church (U.S.A.) are required in the ordination worship service to stand before the body of assembled church members and answer in the affirmative nine questions. The first eight of those questions are asked of all ordination candidates without regard to the office or ministry to which they are being ordained. Only the ninth question is tailored for the responsibilities of a particular ministry.

The first eight questions are a summary of Christian faith and practice. A friend of mine called these questions "a little gem," and indeed they are. The first three questions are theological in nature. Through them one confesses trust in Jesus Christ and the triune God, accepts the Old and New Testaments to be "the unique and authoritative witness to Jesus Christ," and adopts "the essential tenets of the Reformed faith." In answering the fourth question the ordination candidate promises to conduct his or her upcoming ministry as a follower of Jesus Christ, Scripture, and the Reformed confessions. The fifth, sixth, and seventh questions are about church polity and collegial relationships, Christian ethics, and promoting the church's peace, unity, and purity. The candidate promises to conduct her or his ministry accordingly. Then comes the eighth question:

> Will you pray for and seek to serve the people with energy, intelligence, imagination, and love?[40]

---

37. Ibid., 167.
38. Ibid., 210.
39. For a list of the Presbyterian Church (U.S.A.)'s "ordered ministries," their purpose, their qualifications, and a description of the ordination worship service, see *Constitution of the Presbyterian Church (U.S.A.): Part II, Book of Order*, G-2.0102, G-2.0104, and W-4.4000, 25, 25-26, and 121-26.
40. Ibid., W-4.4003h, 123.

Imagination now appears.

Two aspects of imagination in the eighth ordination question stand out. First, every person ordained to an office in the Presbyterian Church (U.S.A.) is called to and expected to be imaginative. Exactly what this means will vary according to the gifts and responsibilities of each person, but the challenge to apply one's gifts and carry out one's responsibilities imaginatively is laid on every candidate for ordination. Second, imagination does not stand alone. It does not function by itself. It appears in the context of prayer, service, work or energy, intelligence, and the ethic of Christian love. It is conducted prayerfully. It is used to serve God and God's people energetically and thoughtfully, loving God and neighbors near and far. Just as imagination stands among colleagues and works with them, so they stand with imagination and work with it. The prayer prays imaginatively. The servant serves imaginatively. The worker works imaginatively. The mind thinks imaginatively. The ethic of love is enacted imaginatively.

But the eighth ordination question is not the only context in which imagination appears. It also appears in the context of all nine ordination questions. Imagination and the church's core theology of trust in Jesus Christ and the triune God, acceptance of the Old and New Testaments as the "authoritative witness to Jesus Christ," and adoption of "the essential tenets of the Reformed faith" are therefore understood to be mutually supportive, not mutually exclusive. Likewise, imagination and key church practices of abiding by the church's polity and discipline, friendship among colleagues in ministry, loving neighbors and working for reconciliation, and promoting the church's peace, unity, and purity are also understood to be mutually supportive, not mutually exclusive. Imagination is a gift of God that can, and often does, serve the faith and practice of Christian communities.

British novelist and lay theologian Sara Maitland affirmed imagination's role in both theology and church life when she wrote:

> The real danger of not treating the creative imagination with real love is that this involves a rejection of God—or at least of a huge and magnificent dimension of God.

Such a rejection seriously impedes the work of religion in the transformation of the world. Any movement for social change requires a revolution of the imagination; and for that, perfect theory is not good enough. There have to be stories told afresh, rhythms created anew, meanings presented to the heart. That is what Jesus' parables are: they aren't just mnemonic aids to good behavior; they are new stories, which construct truths afresh.[41]

Mental Seeing (Continued)

If physical seeing makes possible a range of human experiences, mental seeing makes possible a range of human achievements. Through mental seeing painters visualize new combinations of shapes, objects, colors, scenes, and people on canvas. Through it sculptors visualize new objects or human forms and faces in wood, stone, or other materials. Playwrights and novelists visualize stories, dialogue, and drama in particular locations and circumstances. Poets visualize images, metaphors, and the words that describe them. Architects and engineers visualize buildings, industrial operations, houses, and the functions they will serve; and designers visualize rooms, furniture, technological devices, and how they will be used. Through mental seeing (and sometimes with the help of conceptual imagination) natural scientists imagine hypotheses or experiments in biology, chemistry, or medicine. Through mental seeing (also with the occasional help of conceptual imagination) social scientists imagine behavioral and social constructs, organizational structures, and public policies. Through mental seeing (and with the help of faith traditions) people of faith, theologians, and religious leaders visualize interpretations of ancient texts and understandings of God's actions in a changing world. Like the range of human experiences made possible through physical sight, mental seeing makes possible a vast range of human achievements, so vast that we also dare not underestimate or take for granted this form of vision.

41. Maitland, *Big-Enough God*, 143.

Unlike physical seeing with its limited time perspective, mental seeing may roam freely across time and space. It is not limited to the present moment. It may visualize or imagine objects, scenes, events, or people in the future. It may imagine or visualize an alternative or different present. It may even imagine a past different from one that is said to be historically accurate. To some extent historical fiction is an example of imagining an alternative past. Mental seeing is also not limited to the places seen through visual stimuli. It can relocate objects, scenes, events, and people to a different or alternative location. One of mental seeing's great advantages is that it is not locked into or permanently bound to the present moment or the present location. We have the flexibility to move freely across time and to different places.

Mental seeing, like physical sight, is part of God's creation. It is one of humankind's attributes that God brought into being. Its contribution to human creativity is one, but not the only, reason to think of God's creation as good.[42] Its pervasiveness throughout humankind is a sign of God's love for and kindness toward all human beings. But because it is part of a broken, imperfect creation, it is also fallible and sinful; and its flexibility with respect to time and space provides not only greater freedom, but also more opportunities for participation in human error. Like its counterpart, physical sight, this type of vision lives in the tension between pointing to God's grace and participation in human fallibility.

Because both physical sight and mental seeing are parts of creation and therefore fallible, and because both come from human sources, does God ever use or transform for use these two types of vision? Perhaps. We cannot categorically rule out the possibility. God is certainly able to use and to transform for use our physical and mental visions. But before we jump to the conclusion that God will transform and use our human visions, there are some caveats to consider. First, God does not transform or use every human vision. In fact, we can probably say that God does not transform or use most human visions. Yes, God may do so; but divine ability is not the same as divine action. Second, human visions are never

---

42. Cf. Gen 1.

ideal or error-free. Even though God loves humankind and may choose to transform and use human visions, the visionary and her or his visions remain human. Human visions continue to participate in a fallible world.

In light of these caveats, how can we know whether or when God will choose to use our physical sight or mental seeing? I suggest that we pay attention to Amos Wilder's wise advice, "The Spirit is not to be quenched, yet the spirits should be tested."[43] As we noted earlier, Wilder drew his advice from 1 Thessalonians 5 and 1 John 4. The opening line of 1 John 4 reads, "Beloved, do not believe every spirit, but test the spirits to see whether they are from God." But what tests shall we apply? I recommend two tests. The first is christological: Is our human vision consistent with the person and work of Jesus Christ? The second is canonical: Is our human vision consistent with the biblical witness to God's mission and activity in the world? Admittedly our two tests are imprecise and not guaranteed to yield absolute clarity, but they are possible starting points for deeper reflection on our visions.

In truth, we human beings can only offer our physical and mental visions to God. We cannot summon God to use them or to confirm what we think we are seeing. God will choose whether or not to transform, use, or confirm our visions. We are called first and foremost to trust God and obey God, called to a faith that "is the assurance of things hoped for, the conviction of things not seen."[44]

Revelatory Seeing: Vision as Disclosure

The third mode or form of seeing is revelatory seeing. In contrast to physical sight and mental seeing, both of which originate within human beings, this third mode or form originates from an external source, a source outside of human beings, namely, from God. The divine origin of revelatory seeing is its chief characteristic.

---

43. Wilder, *Theopoetic*, 22.
44. Heb 11:1.

God and God alone, in this form of seeing, reveals something or discloses something to a vision's recipient(s).

Some people confuse revelatory seeing with their feelings. Feelings are inferences or intuitions based on human experiences, experiences that are sometimes limited. They are generated within and among human beings. And they are related to the imagination and may at times be connected to mental seeing.[45] All that we have previously said about imagination and mental seeing may apply to feelings. But, our feelings are not necessarily God's direct disclosure. They reveal at best the human mind and heart that expresses them.

Meanwhile some people speak of revelatory seeing as "religious vision" or "spiritual vision." Unfortunately, the adjectives "religious" and "spiritual" have become quite general in their meanings. Either word may mean any of the following: devout, pious, godly, holy, saintly, reverent, righteous, good, or pure. Either may be used to describe personal or communal disciplines such as prayer or worship. Either may be used to describe certain doctrines, beliefs, or ethical standards. The word "religious" can mean fervent, zealous, or even self-righteous; and the word "spiritual" can mean incorporeal, nonmaterial, unearthly, ghostly, or mystic. At present, "religious" seems to be the word of choice when referring to church institutions and their practices. With so many different word meanings, phrases such as "religious vision" and "spiritual seeing" are ambiguous at best and misleading at worst. The third form of seeing requires the more precise vocabulary found in the verbs "reveal" and "disclose" and their accompanying nouns (revelation, disclosure) and adjectives (revelatory, disclosive).

While physical sight and mental seeing are parts of God's creation, revelatory seeing, vision as disclosure, is part of God's special revelation.[46] We call this revelation "special" because it is God's self-revelation. God is disclosing to the world who God is and what God has done and is doing in the world. This self-dis-

---

45. Bryant, *Faith and the Play of Imagination*, 204–5.

46. For a summary of the doctrine of special revelation, see Guthrie, *Christian Doctrine*, 53–69.

closure comes to us in three ways: (1) in God's words and actions in history, especially in the person and work of Jesus Christ; (2) in the biblical witness to God's words, actions, and promises in history and in Jesus Christ; and (3) in the community of people, past and present, who have proclaimed and lived by faith in Jesus Christ and in accord with the biblical witness. We shall look briefly at each of the three ways.

God's primary means of self-disclosure was and is through Jesus Christ. Matthew's Gospel attests to the revelatory importance of Jesus' birth when it cites a text from Isaiah 7:14 and then interprets that text's key word, Emmanuel:

> "[A]nd they shall name him Emmanuel," which means, "God is with us."[47]

Paul in his letter to the Philippians attests to God's self-disclosure in Jesus' crucifixion when he remembers an early church hymn that speaks of Jesus Christ:

> who, though he was in the form of God,
> > did not regard equality with God
> > as something to be exploited,
> but emptied himself,
> > taking the form of a slave,
> > being born in human likeness.
> And being found in human form,
> > he humbled himself
> > and became obedient to the point of death—
> > even death on a cross.[48]

But it is John's Gospel that most clearly identifies Jesus Christ as God's self-revelation:

> In the beginning was the Word, and the Word was with God, and the Word was God. He was in the beginning with God. . . . And the Word became flesh and lived

---

47. Matt 1:23.
48. Phil 2:6–8.

among us. . . . No one has ever seen God. It is the only Son . . . who has made him known.[49]

Based on the testimony from John's Gospel, we often refer to Jesus Christ as "God's Word made flesh" or "the Word of God incarnate." Furthermore, God's primary means of self-revelation in Jesus Christ is the basis for the christological test mentioned in the previous section.

The second way in which God discloses God's self is through the biblical witness. The Bible's vision narratives, for example, are not merely stories from the past. They are part of the biblical witness and part of God's self-revelation to us today. Through these stories we learn that God is the source of vision, that God's visions are about multiple and multifaceted subjects, that God's visions are not limited to one time perspective, that God alone chooses visions' recipients, and that God's visions often point us to or prepare us for something greater than we can imagine. Moreover, other biblical texts complement the Bible's vision stories. From these texts we learn that no one, not even the powerless, is outside the scope of God's vision or the range of God's grace; that God's vision of the future is a vision of hospitality for all in worship, instruction, justice, and peace; that the gifts of the Spirit, prophecy, dreams, and visions, are available to both sexes, all ages, and all classes; that Jesus both challenges our failure to see and grants our desires to see God at work among us; and that where there is no vision, confusion will reign among people.

We often refer to these stories and texts, together with other parts of the biblical witness, as "the Word of God written." They are secondary to God's primary self-disclosure in Jesus Christ; but even though they are secondary, God still reveals God's self through them. And they are the basis for the canonical test also mentioned in the previous section.

The third way by which God reveals God's self is in the community of God's faithful people, the church. In many respects the church is a human organization like every other human

---

49. John 1:1–2, 14, 18.

organization. In it humanity's fallibility and failures are on display. Church history has had its dark moments and movements, even moments of complicity with some of the world's worst evil.

Nevertheless, there have been and are moments and movements through which God disclosed and discloses God's self to people and to the world. In the church's preaching and teaching we may hear and study God's Word, preaching and teaching that we refer to as "the Word of God proclaimed." In the church's worship, prayer, and liturgy, we are brought face to face with God's holiness and astonishing love. In the church's mission in our communities and around the world, we see God's own mission to those in need of both food and the gospel. Through the church's people who nurtured and befriended us, we heard and hear God's call to service and leadership. Together with the church's people, we catch glimpses—even visions—of God's challenges before us; and together we test the spirits with our christological and canonical tests to clarify and confirm, as best we can, the reality of what God has disclosed.

John 9 and Forms of Seeing

Seeing is undoubtedly one of the themes in the story of the man born blind.[50] For the story's vocabulary of seeing is much too pervasive to ignore. Verbs meaning "see" and the adjective "blind," the opposite of seeing, appear from the beginning of the story to its end. The noun "eyes," the expression "open one's eyes," and a verb meaning "receive or restore one's sight" are quite common in the story. Even the important phrase "light of the world" at the beginning of the story[51] and the key word "judgment" near the story's end[52] are related to the theme of seeing. For light enables seeing; and seeing enables judgment, a reference to a judicial-like decision that distinguishes or separates believers from unbelievers.[53] The story of the

---

50. John 9:1–41.
51. John 9:5.
52. John 9:39.
53. Bauer et al., *Greek-English Lexicon*, 452.

man born blind does have other themes; but the theme of seeing is an ever-present, not-to-be-disregarded element in the story.

Furthermore, just as seeing is a theme in the story of the man born blind, so the story also depicts the various forms of seeing or the absence thereof. When I say "depicts," I am not saying that John 9 was written for the purpose of defining the various forms of seeing. To the contrary, it was written for an entirely different purpose, namely, a christological purpose. It is "John's conception of the work of Christ."[54] However, in the course of expressing his conception of Christ's work through the story of the man born blind, the gospel writer indicates that he understands there are various types of seeing; and he illustrates the various types, or absence thereof, as he tells the story. He presupposes the various types without explicitly defining them.

Some literary features of the story are worth noting. John 9 is mostly a series of dialogues or conversations. The dialogues carry the story, and most of the story's key lines are words exchanged between and among the story's speakers. Narrative plays a less important role in the story. It supplies a few essential details and provides a bridge or transition from one scene in the story to another. John 9 is almost, but not quite, a brief one-act play.

If we were to rewrite John 9 as a one-act play, the play would organize itself into five scenes: verses 1–7, 8–12, 13–23, 24–34, and 35–41. Each scene has its own cast of characters. The man born blind is the only character who appears in all five scenes. Jesus appears in the first scene and in the final scene, and the timing of his appearances is significant. The disciples appear only in the first scene. Neighbors appear only in the second, and the parents of the man born blind appear only in the third. Pharisees appear in scenes 3, 4, and 5. We will look now at each scene.

The first scene opens with Jesus' sighting of the man born blind and the disciples asking who had sinned, the man or his parents. The disciples' question presupposed a belief, commonly held at that time, that illness and physical disability were the result of sin. Jesus denied that either the man or his parents had sinned and

---

54. Barrett, *Gospel According to St. John*, 293.

instead pointed to a far more important role and purpose for the man born blind:

> [H]e was born blind so that God's works might be revealed in him. We must work the works of him who sent me while it is day.... As long as I am in the world, I am the light of the world.[55]

The blind man's role and purpose was to make known the works of God, to show the effects of "the light of the world" upon the surrounding world and people.

Furthermore, Jesus did not merely talk about God's works and "the light of the world." He proceeded immediately, without being asked, to give sight to the man who had been blind from birth. He put his words into action. He spat on the ground, made mud, spread the mud on the blind man's eyes, and told him to wash in the pool of Siloam. The blind man went, washed, and "came back able to see."[56] Scene 1 ends with the man born blind having received his physical eyesight, the first form of seeing. It ends with "the light of the world" having given light to one whose entire life to that point had been spent in darkness.

In scene 2 the man born blind was back in his old neighborhood, and the neighbors were talking. "Isn't this the man who used to sit and beg?" they asked.[57] "How were your eyes opened?" The formerly blind man responded in detail, telling how Jesus made mud, put it on his eyes, and told him to go to Siloam and wash. "Where is [Jesus]?" they wanted to know.[58] The neighbors doubted that a blind-from-birth man could ever receive his eyesight.

Scene 3 continues the dialogue begun in scene 2, but with a new cast of characters, Pharisees and parents instead of neighbors, and with new information that Jesus had opened the blind man's eyes on the Sabbath. The Pharisees began by repeating the question the neighbors had asked, namely, how had the man born blind

---

55. John 9:3b–5.
56. John 9:7.
57. John 9:8b.
58. John 9:12.

received his sight? The man gave a straightforward answer, but the Pharisees were more interested in debating among themselves over Jesus' healing on the Sabbath than in the man's answer. When their debate ended inconclusively, they asked him, "What do you say about [Jesus]?" The man replied, "He is a prophet."[59]

Refusing to believe that the man was in fact born blind and had only recently received his sight, the Pharisees summoned the man's parents. The parents asserted that the man was indeed their son and that he had in fact been born blind, but they carefully denied any knowledge of how he had received his sight or who had opened his eyes because of their fear of the Jewish authorities. The parents concluded their testimony by passing the buck back to their son: "Ask him; he is of age. He will speak for himself."[60]

Scene 4 is a tense, conflicted dialogue between the man born blind and the Pharisees who summoned him to a second meeting. To the Pharisees assertion that Jesus was a sinner, the man born blind replied, "I do not know whether he is a sinner. One thing I do know, that though I was blind, now I see."[61] The dialogue continued with greater emotional intensity:

> Pharisees: How did he open your eyes?
>
> Man: I have told you already, and you would not listen. Why do you want to hear it again? Do you want to become his disciples?
>
> Pharisees: You are his disciple, but we are disciples of Moses. We know that God has spoken to Moses, but as for this man, we do not know where he comes from.
>
> Man: Here is an astonishing thing! You do not know where he comes from, and yet he opened my eyes. We know that God does not listen to sinners, but he does listen to one who worships him and obeys his will. Never since the world began has

---

59. John 9:17.
60. John 9:21.
61. John 9:25.

it been heard that anyone opened the eyes of a person born blind. If this man were not from God, he could do nothing.

Pharisees: You were born entirely in sins, and are you trying to teach us?[62]

Scene 4 ends with the Pharisees driving the man born blind out of the synagogue.

If we look back at scenes 2, 3, and 4 together, two features of the story come into view. One is the absence of the second form of seeing, mental vision, among the neighbors and among the Pharisees. The neighbors' questions were signs of their lack of imagination, signs of their inability to visualize the man born blind as anything other than a blind beggar. The neighbors could not see new possibilities for their once familiar street beggar or for themselves. Likewise, the Pharisees' questions, assertions, and arguments were also signs of their lack of imagination. They could not imagine that one who healed on the Sabbath could be anything more than a sinner or that one born blind could receive his sight. They could not visualize the possibility that God might speak or act after or beyond Moses. The questions, declarations, and contentions of the neighbors and the Pharisees were the antithesis of mental vision.

The second noteworthy feature of scenes 2, 3, and 4 is the gradual growth of the man born blind. In scene 2 when the neighbors asked him where Jesus was, he answered simply, "I do not know."[63] In scene 3 when the Pharisees asked what he would say about Jesus, he answered, "He is a prophet."[64] In scene 4, however, he made some bold statements about what he had experienced and about Jesus. When told Jesus was a sinner, he responded, "I do not know whether he is a sinner. One thing I do know, that though I was blind, now I see."[65] When asked what Jesus did to him, he noted that he had already answered the question and then added, "Why do you want to hear it again? Do you want to become

62. John 9:26–34a.
63. John 9:12.
64. John 9:17.
65. John 9:25.

his disciples?"[66] And when the Pharisees asserted that they were disciples of Moses, the man born blind challenged them with a response that began and ended as follows: "Here is an astonishing thing! . . . Never since the world began has it been heard that anyone opened the eyes of a person born blind. If this man were not from God, he could do nothing."[67] Although the story does not explain it clearly, the man born blind was gradually changing.

In the fifth and final scene Jesus re-enters the story and finds the man born blind. Jesus took the initiative; and when he found him, he asked, "Do you believe in the Son of Man?"[68] The man replied, "And who is he, sir? Tell me, so that I may believe in him."[69] And Jesus answered, "You have seen him, and the one speaking with you is he."[70] With these words the man who had once been a blind beggar received divine self-disclosure. He became the recipient of the third form of seeing, revelatory seeing, when Jesus identified himself as the Son of Man; and the man responded with a final bold confession, "I believe," and with worship.[71]

The man born blind's part in the story is now complete, but the final scene isn't over yet. Jesus summarizes the meaning of the story in words that should be understood in conjunction with his opening words in scene 1[72] and with the story's christological purpose: "I came into this world for judgment so that those who do not see may see, and those who do see may become blind."[73] Jesus was saying that he came as "the light of the world" to distinguish those who are blind and know they need "light" from those who think they see but do not. Some of the Pharisees overheard Jesus comment and said to him, "Surely we are not blind, are we?"[74]

66. John 9:27.
67. John 9:30, 32–33.
68. John 9:35.
69. John 9:36.
70. John 9:37
71. John 9:38.
72. John 9:3–5.
73. John 9:39.
74. John 9:40.

Jesus replied in words consistent with his previous statement: "If you were blind, you would not have sin. But now that you say, 'We see,' your sin remains."[75] A colleague of mine commented on the ending of John 9 in words worth pondering. "Blindness," he said, "is a precondition for seeing."

Visioning in Practice: A Note to Church Leaders

In theory we have made distinctions among three types of vision. In practice, however, the boundaries among them are not absolute and not always clear. Exactly when does sensory vision become mental vision? When exactly does mental vision or visual imagination become revelatory seeing or vision as disclosure, or vice versa? And what are the relationships and the boundaries between any of the three modes or forms of seeing and our auditory imagination, our conceptual imagination, our traditions, or our feelings? What may have seemed clear in theory can suddenly feel ambiguous in practice.

Rather than thinking of the boundaries among the three forms of seeing as fixed, clear, and distinct, I recommend that we, when using any of the forms, consider their boundaries to be porous, permeable, much like membranes. Perhaps neuroscientists have the right idea when they lump perceptions, memories, and concepts into one ambiguous category called "working memory." After all, our God-given brains are quite capable of using multiple types of vision at the same time.

I also recommend that we consider the following when using any of the three vision types or forms of seeing in church practice.

We need all three modes or forms of seeing, all three types of vision; and we need every time perspective: past, present, and future. There is no hierarchy of vision types. One type is not more valuable than the others. Each vision type is valuable to human well-being, although each contributes something different to human well-being. As noted earlier in the chapter, physical sight makes possible a

---

75. John 9:41.

range of human experiences, while mental vision or visual imagination makes possible a range of human achievements. And vision as disclosure reveals something about God, aspects of God's nature or God's actions in the world. We should resist the temptation to reduce vision to, for example, mental seeing or visual imagination. For we need the ability to observe the immediate, concrete realities around us and the ability to discern God's past and present work in the world, just as much as we need our visual imagination.

Similarly, there is no hierarchy of time perspectives. Visions are not limited to only one time, for example, the future. Those who clearly see the present, who clearly see the dynamics and significance of contemporary events and movements, are as much visionaries as those who dream of the future. And those who see the past and how the past is affecting the present are also as much visionaries as those who predict the future. In visioning we should resist the temptation to speak only in the future tense. In some circumstances speaking of the past or present requires as much imagination as envisioning the future.

Start visioning with immersion in the Bible's stories and texts about vision. Start with the authoritative witness to Jesus Christ, who was and is divine disclosure.[76] Ponder the notion that God is the source of vision in these stories and texts and the meaning of that notion for human visions. Consider the variety of visions' subjects in these stories and texts and the contrast between this diversity and the limited organizational focus in today's vision statements. Note the diversity of time perspectives in these stories and texts vis-à-vis today's singular focus on the future. Observe visions' recipients in these stories and texts, including the powerless, the blind, sinners, or entire communities and nations. Would we have chosen these particular recipients, and what does the choice of recipients say about God and about us? Ponder the purpose of each vision in the Bible's stories and texts. In what ways do these purposes challenge the purposes of our human visions, or offer us hope, or reveal to us the presence and nature of God? Is the gift of vision really available to us now? And to what extent is our confusion the absence of vision?

---

76. *Constitution of the Presbyterian Church (U.S.A.)*, W-4.4003b, 122.

Toward Understanding Vision

Beginning with the Bible's stories and texts about vision places our visioning process in the context of our faith traditions and empowers our traditions to speak to us throughout the process.

When speaking of vision and visioning processes, we should, to the extent possible, identify the form(s) of seeing, the vision type(s) we are using, and their source(s). In observing, for example, trends and movements in contemporary church life, we are using our physical sight, a human source of vision. In imagining new ways of ministering to people, new congregations or worshipping communities, or new forms of mission in our region or the world, we are using our mental vision, also a human source of vision. When we base our imagination on our feelings, we are continuing to use our mental vision; but when we base it on our faith traditions, we have opened ourselves to the possibility of revelatory seeing, the possibility of divine disclosure. As noted in a previous paragraph, the distinctions in practice among the types of vision are not always clear or easily made. Nevertheless, in the interest of greater clarity, we should try to identify the type(s) and sources(s) of our vision. Clarity lessens, and sometimes avoids altogether, confusion and exaggerated claims about vision and visioning; and on the positive side, it promotes modesty and precision of thought in our use of vision and visioning.

Beware of promises that we can definitively see or know the future. We can hope for a particular future; and indeed I and many others believe that hope is a prerequisite for any visioning of the future. We can plan for a future, provided we acknowledge that plans can and do go awry. We can sometimes influence the future, but not always and not in all circumstances. We can even predict or forecast the future, in the sense that we can state what we believe will happen in the future, but we cannot guarantee the accuracy of our forecasts. Physically seeing the future or knowing the future with absolute certainty are beyond the limits of our humanity. Claims or promises that we can physically see or know with certainty the future are exaggerated at best and at worst completely false.

In church settings our visions that come from a human source should be realistic, modest, and also challenging, but not grandiose

Old Man Dreaming

or triumphal.[77] I grant that there is some tension between realistic and modest on the one hand and challenging on the other. My experience, however, is that in any meaningful vision people need both a connection to reality and a challenge to grow beyond that reality. People seem to yearn for the safety and security of something familiar while also yearning for the adventure of the new and creative. Without a connection to reality they feel uprooted and lost. Without challenge they become bored and apathetic. Meaningful visions find a balance between the two.

What we do not need in church settings are grandiose or triumphal visions, visions characterized by grandeur, splendor, size and scope that exceed ordinary experience, or inflated pretensions and egos. We get enough of such visions from the surrounding culture and need not increase their number. Our visions should instead be modest; they should be consistent with our beliefs and traditions, our ministries and mission—visions consistent with the God whom we worship and serve. And our visions should be appropriate to the particular settings that we are called to serve, whether those settings are congregations, judicatories, church institutions, whole denominations, or ecumenical and international agencies.

We should study and weigh visions and practice visioning in a spirit of "fear and trembling." The phrase "fear and trembling" appears in both Corinthian letters, Ephesians, and Philippians. In each of these contexts, the word "fear" refers to reverence or respect; and the phrase "fear and trembling" implies awe, wonder, and humility. "Fear and trembling" is the opposite of arrogance or dominance; and as such, it can free a person and a community from prejudice and presuppositions and open the eyes to accurate perceptions, the mind to imaginative thoughts, and the heart and soul to all that God discloses.

---

77. For a discussion of how American Protestants might offer a non-triumphal public witness in a pluralistic society, see McBride, *Church for the World*.

7

A Vision for the Presbyterian Church (U.S.A.)

Part 1: Seeing the Present

I'M OLD. As I write these words, I am in the eighth decade of life.

For a long time I've been dreaming—dreaming like the "old men" whom the prophet Joel mentioned and to whom the apostle Peter referred at Pentecost: "Your old men shall dream dreams."[1] For me, this means dreaming in the sense of reflecting upon, thinking about, imagining, or visualizing—dreaming about my church, the Presbyterian Church (U.S.A.), about what I perceive to be its present state, and about its future or at least the future I hope to see.

I believe that God has promised to and does walk with us in the present and into the unknown and the unforeseeable. In that spirit, I offer two chapters' thoughts on the present and future of the Presbyterian Church (U.S.A.).

In chapter 6 I contended that those who see the dynamics and significance of contemporary events and movements are as much visionaries as those who dream of the future. I also contended that speaking of the present might require as much imagination as

---

1. Joel 2:28; Acts 2:17.

envisioning the future. Michael Jinkins, citing Martin Luther King Jr., John Calvin, and G. K. Chesterton, seems to agree:

> Both King and Calvin call for an engagement with the reality of the church that ordinarily lies in our path rather than with an imaginary, idealistic church that exists only in abstract ratiocination—an engagement that requires of us what G. K. Chesterton once described as that most soaring variety of imagination, the imagination to see what is really there. What we require, then, is the imagination to speak clearly about what it means when we speak of the church ordinarily.[2]

After some comments on the current religious and philosophical context, I will speak of *my* church ordinarily using four complementary images.

In a Secular Age

Of the many ways of describing American Christianity's context, one that is clearly important, and often overlooked, is a description of the philosophical and religious milieu surrounding churches and Christians in the U.S. An exemplar of such a description is *A Secular Age* by Canadian philosopher Charles Taylor, a book that one scholar called "one of the most important books of the new millennium."[3]

In *A Secular Age* Taylor identifies three types of secularity. The first type, which he named "secularity 1," is the freeing of certain public areas and institutions, usually political institutions, from connection to or adherence to God or particular religious practices. Religion thus becomes a private matter.[4] Through the adoption of the First Amendment to the Constitution, with its prohibition of religious "establishment" and its guarantee of religious "free exercise," and the legal doctrine of church-state separation, secularity 1 was effectively accomplished in the U.S. Secularity 2 is

---

2. Jinkins, *Church Faces Death*, 87.
3. T. Smith, Review of *How (Not) to Be Secular*, 42.
4. Taylor, *Secular Age*, 1–2.

A Vision ... Part One: Seeing the Present

a decline in religious belief and practice, presumably powered by the rise of other beliefs such as faith in science or reason.[5] Secularity 3 is a change in the conditions of belief, a shift "from a society where belief in God is unchallenged . . . to one in which it is understood to be one option among others."[6] Secularity 3 is Taylor's primary interest, an interest apparent in his key question:

> Why was it virtually impossible not to believe in God in, say, 1500 in our Western society, while in 2000 many of us find this not only easy, but even inescapable?[7]

In *A Secular Age* Taylor answers his own question by telling the story of secularization's appearance and rise in Western society and by his critical analysis of secularization.

Taylor begins his story with three medieval assumptions that made belief in God seem undeniable: (1) the natural world, even storms, droughts, and plagues, testifies to divine purpose and action; (2) social and political orders are grounded in a higher, divine reality; and (3) people are open to and enchanted by spirits, demons, moral forces, and magic.[8] Although Renaissance humanism and various social and religious reform movements had challenged these assumptions before 1500, it was the Protestant Reformation that overturned them. Luther's proclamation of salvation by faith alone and of the priesthood of all believers undermined both the fear of enchantment and the fear of hierarchical power that had separated clergy and laity in the Catholic Church.[9] And John Calvin and Calvinists energized additional disenchantment and the drive to reorder all of society, not merely church structures.[10]

Today's leaders of churches in the Reformed tradition should pay attention to Taylor's comments on Calvin and Calvinists, because the unintended consequence of increased disenchantment

---

5. Ibid., 2, 4.
6. Ibid., 3.
7. Ibid., 25.
8. Ibid., 25.
9. Ibid., 74–75.
10. Ibid., 75–84.

and the drive to reorder all of society was that a disengaged, rational, disciplined stance toward self and society became the defining feature of modern identity. Taylor called this stance "the buffered self," meaning a self that is buffered against a fear of spirits, demons, magic, or external forces.[11] He also noted the irony that "so much of the fruit of devotion and faith prepares the ground for an escape from faith into a purely immanent world."[12]

Although the Reformation broke the medieval barriers to unbelief and introduced disenchantment, societal reform, and the buffered self into Western society, a purely immanent, non-transcendent alternative to Christian belief did not emerge until deism appeared in the late seventeenth and early eighteenth centuries. Taylor identifies three facets of deism that generated a non-transcendent alternative. The first was a narrowing or a reduction in the purposes of God's providence, "an anthropocentric shift" from God's manifold purposes for humankind to a single "economic" order of mutual human benefit. Taylor calls this shift, this narrowing, "Providential Deism."[13]

The second facet was "a drift away from orthodox Christian conceptions of God as an agent interacting with humans and intervening in human history, and towards God as architect of a universe operating by unchanging laws, which humans have to conform to or suffer the consequences."[14] Taylor refers to this facet as "the slide to impersonal order."[15] The third facet was "the idea of a true, original natural religion" that is open to rational scrutiny, but not to forms of personal relation between Creator and creatures.[16]

Through these facets of deism, "an exclusive humanism became a live option for large numbers of people, first among elites,

---

11. Ibid., 134–37.
12. Ibid., 145.
13. Ibid., 221–24, 290.
14. Ibid., 270.
15. Ibid., 292.
16. Ibid., 221, 292–93.

and then more generally."[17] Taylor defines exclusive humanism and its relationship to secularity:

> The coming of modern secularity in my sense has been coterminous with the rise of a society in which for the first time in history a purely self-sufficient humanism came to be a widely available option. I mean by this a humanism accepting no final goal beyond human flourishing, nor any allegiance to anything else beyond this flourishing.[18]

> A secular age is one in which the eclipse of all goals beyond human flourishing becomes conceivable; or better, it falls within the range of an imaginable life for masses of people. This is the crucial link between secularity and a self-sufficient humanism.[19]

Taylor continues his story of exclusive humanism and secularity 3 into the nineteenth and twentieth centuries. He notes "an ever-widening variety of moral/spiritual options," including additional modes of unbelief, and the rise of a "culture of 'authenticity,' or expressive individualism" in Western societies.[20] "We are now living," he writes, "in a spiritual super-nova, a kind of galloping pluralism on the spiritual plane."[21]

Reading Charles Taylor's *A Secular Age* is a daunting task. His book is long (776 pages plus 73 pages of notes). He often returns to and rethinks earlier themes, and he uses technical terms and phrases that are not familiar to ordinary readers. To make Taylor's ideas more accessible, James K. A. Smith has written what he calls "a small field guide" to Taylor's book.[22] Smith's guide includes a helpful glossary of Taylor's terms and phrases.

Whether one reads Taylor or reads Smith about Taylor or studies Taylor's ideas by another method, it is essential that American church leaders understand and be conversant with the major

17. Ibid., 221.
18. Ibid., 18.
19. Ibid., 19–20.
20. Ibid., 299.
21. Ibid., 300.
22. J. Smith, *How (Not) to Be Secular*, ix.

themes in Taylor's book. For Taylor's themes are not purely theoretical, even though he uses philosophical terms. His themes are about concepts that arose in human history and continue to affect the lives and thoughts of human beings today. American Christians and churches now exist in a secular age. Under the influence of modern science and technology, the disenchantment begun in the Reformation continues. In the political rhetoric of our time, we can hear echoes of the drive for societal reform in phrases like "welfare reform, tax reform, healthcare reform, and immigration reform." The rational, disciplined, buffered self remains a feature of modern identity. And in our congregations we can encounter people whose idea of God has been reduced to a cosmic architect of a universe operating by unchanging laws or whose conception of God's providence is limited to an economic order of mutual human benefit. An exclusive, self-sufficient humanism is no longer limited to a few elites; it is now the religion of choice for a growing segment of the U.S. population.

Taylor's ideas help American Christians understand the philosophical and religious context surrounding them; why their churches feel beleaguered and their faith feels contested (and it is being contested); and why the "nones," those who claim no religious affiliation, are increasing. On a positive note, his ideas also help Christians differentiate themselves from exclusive humanists and clarify their own beliefs and identity. Understanding Taylor's ideas is difficult, but we should not ignore them.

An Anxious Family

When I look at the Presbyterian Church (U.S.A.), I see an anxious family, an image drawn from family systems theory and family therapy.

Family theorists and therapists make a distinction between acute and chronic anxiety:

> Acute anxiety generally occurs in response to real threats and is experienced as time-limited. People usually adapt to acute anxiety fairly successfully. Chronic anxiety

generally occurs in response to imagined threats and is not experienced as time-limited. Chronic anxiety often strains or exceeds people's ability to adapt to it. Acute anxiety is fed by fear of what is; chronic anxiety is fed by fear of what might be.[23]

Rabbi and therapist Edwin Friedman embraced the distinction between acute and chronic anxiety and elaborated extensively on chronic anxiety. "It is a regressive emotional process,"[24] he said. "The issues over which chronically anxious systems become concerned" are seldom the real causes of anxiety, and "quick-fix technical solutions" to anxiety seldom work.[25] In fact, continued Friedman, most individuals and most social systems will "choose or revert to chronic conditions of bearable pain rather than face the temporarily more intense anguish of acute conditions that are the gateway to becoming free."[26]

Friedman identified and defined five interlocking characteristics of chronically anxious families:

1. Reactivity, a "vicious cycle of intense reactions" among family members.
2. Herding, in which "the forces for togetherness triumph over the forces for individuality."
3. Blaming, "rather than taking responsibility for their own being and destiny."
4. A quick-fix mentality that "seeks symptom relief rather than fundamental change."
5. Lack of well-differentiated leadership, "a failure of nerve that both stems from and contributes to the first four."[27]

---

23. Kerr and Bowen, *Family Evaluation*, 113.
24. Friedman, *Failure of Nerve*, 58.
25. Ibid., 59.
26. Ibid., 60–61.
27. Ibid., 53–54.

Friedman argued that the first four of these characteristics both pervert an evolutionary principle and have a negative effect on leadership.[28] Reactivity perverts the self-regulation of instinctual drives and "wears leaders down by sabotaging their initiatives and resolve with constant automatic responses."[29] Herding perverts adaptation to strength; it makes leaders indecisive and promotes their appeasement of troublesome people. Blaming distorts responses to challenge, to the point that those most capable of leading do not seek leadership positions. A quick-fix mentality perverts the principle that maturation takes time and undermines a leader's opportunity and capacity to grow.

Friedman did not limit his five characteristics to anxious families. He saw clearly the presence and effects of the same characteristics in American society as a whole and in its institutions and organizations, including churches and synagogues. He underscored for us the parallels between chronically anxious families and our chronically anxious society with its anxious organizations and institutions.[30]

Using the concepts of family theorists and therapists, especially Friedman's, examples and contours of anxiety in the Presbyterian Church (U.S.A.) come readily into view. Some of our anxiety is, to be sure, acute. When, for instance, we experience specific losses—losses of friends and fellow church members to death or movement, reductions in a congregation's financial resources, changes in or dissolution of favorite programs or ministries, church closings, and departures or retirements of beloved pastors or church leaders—we feel the pain of our losses, mourn accordingly, and eventually adapt to our new circumstances.

Unfortunately much of our anxiety is chronic anxiety. What church leader has not felt the wrath of church members or volunteers who overreact to an action or decision with which they disagree? Who has not felt pressure to "join with our friends" in supporting or opposing a proposal before a church council, a proposal

28. Ibid., 61, 91–92, 94.
29. Ibid., 64.
30. Ibid., 61–94.

about which one may have misgivings? What church leader has not been blamed for an event or phenomenon over which she or he has no control? A church member once blamed me and my church executive colleagues for a proposal before the General Assembly, a proposal that we neither wrote nor submitted and that the Assembly never adopted. And I long ago stopped counting the one-size-fits-all evangelism, stewardship, youth ministry, and other programs that someone promised would solve particular church problems. Such experiences illustrate that chronic anxiety and its characteristics do indeed affect the Presbyterian Church (U.S.A.).

As we Presbyterians and others ponder the image of ourselves as an anxious family, we could also reflect on some of Scripture's words about fear and anxiety. Psalm writers assert, "With the Lord on my side I do *not fear*,"[31] and, "Yea, though I walk through the valley of the shadow of death, I will *fear no evil*; for thou art with me."[32] According to Luke, angels of the Lord began their messages to Zechariah, Mary, and the shepherds with the plea: "Do *not be afraid*."[33] And Jesus in the Sermon on the Mount entreats us, "Do *not be anxious* about your life, what you shall eat or what you shall drink, nor about your body, what you shall put on. . . . Do *not be anxious* about tomorrow."[34] These and other biblical texts seem to understand our fearfulness and at the same time prod us gently to move away from anxiety and toward trust in God.

A Fractured Body

When I observe the Presbyterian Church (U.S.A.), I see a fractured body.

The decisions of some congregations and members to leave the Presbyterian Church (U.S.A.) are ample evidence of our fracturing. Most of the departed describe themselves as evangelicals,

---

31. Ps 118:6.
32. Ps 23:4.
33. Luke 1:13, 30; 2:10.
34. Matt 6:25, 34.

and their rationale for departure has usually been the Presbyterian Church's decisions to permit the ordination of gays and lesbians and the marriage of same-sex couples. The departing congregations include some of our denomination's largest.

But we should not assume that our fracturing is a recent or unique event. Reformed churches have a long history of church splits, a history that extends back to the sixteenth century. Neither should we blame one particular group for our fracturing. Instead, self-examination and acceptance of responsibility, not blaming, should be our response to fracturing. Nor should we assume that our fracturing is merely the result of controversies around homosexuality. Other issues besides homosexuality have vexed and continue to vex us, thus guaranteeing us divided votes and dissenting voices in the foreseeable future.

Also, without most of us knowing it, our internal fracturing has occurred within the context of an American society and culture that has been breaking itself into smaller and smaller units. Historian Daniel T. Rodgers described American intellectual history in the period between 1970 and 2000 as a shift from large, unifying, collective ideas to smaller, weaker, more fragmented notions. Wrote Rodgers:

> Strong metaphors of society were supplanted by weaker ones. Imagined collectives shrank; notions of structure and power thinned out. Viewed by its acts of mind, the last quarter of the century was an era of disaggregation, a great age of fracture.[35]

Rodgers analyzed Ronald Reagan's major speeches and noted that Reagan and his speechwriters intentionally refashioned presidential rhetoric from Cold War themes of national resolve to themes of individual freedom.[36] He also analyzed changes in economic thought; concepts of power, race, and gender; notions of society and justice; and ideas about history. He observed shifts from Keynesian economics to market economics, from big social structures

---

35. Rodgers, *Age of Fracture*, 3.
36. Ibid., 15–40.

A Vision ... Part One: Seeing the Present

and interest groups to "smaller and actor-centered dimensions," and from a unified black memory and identity to "fissures within African-American society."[37] By the twentieth century's end, according to Rodgers, there had been a "destabilization of gender roles and gender certainties"; "the idea of equality had lost its urgency"; and the idea of history as a common narrative had given way to history as ideological, apocalyptic, and showing "original intent."[38]

If the twentieth century ended with fissures in American cultural and intellectual life, the twenty-first century has seen increasing polarization in American politics. A Pew research study confirmed the trend toward increasing ideological and partisan polarization, and a news report summarized some of the Pew study's findings:

> The animosity [between liberals and conservatives] is so deep that many would be unhappy if a close relative married someone of a different political persuasion.
>
> The survey shows that liberals and conservatives have self-segregating preferences, with many explicitly preferring to live around people with similar political views, and others expressing preferences that indirectly lead them toward communities dominated by their fellow partisans.[39]

The 2016 general election and its aftermath attested to the depth of the political divide in the United States.

Although no one argues that cultural fragmentation and political polarization cause church fracturing, it is certainly possible for such fragmentation and polarization to influence church members' behavior, and nowhere more so than in the Presbyterian Church (U.S.A.). Presbyterians, both as a group and as individuals, are often attuned to contemporary ideas, values, and trends and sometimes are the leaders of such ideas, values, and trends. Under these circumstances we Presbyterians were surely affected by the late twentieth century's social and cultural fracturing, and

---

37. Ibid., 109–10, 143.
38. Ibid., 145, 220, 232–42.
39. Cohn, "Polarization Is Dividing American Society."

we are surely being affected by the twenty-first century's political polarization.

But, as we consider our fractured body, let us note some glimmers of hope. When we remain together as a church, as many of us have; when we refuse to follow the pied pipers of division; when we take seriously Jesus' prayer on behalf of believers "that they may be one"[40]; when we continue to profess our faith in "one holy catholic and apostolic church"; when we confess our sin and acknowledge our complicity in the ongoing divisions in Christianity; when we work for the reconciliation of the church and the world—when we do any or all of these, we are a countercultural witness in our community and world, a witness that stands against the forces of fracture and polarization and declares that they shall not have the last word.

Gifted Members

When I view the Presbyterian Church (U.S.A.), I see gifted members, who are a strength for the church, but not a panacea.

I marvel at the range of talent among Presbyterians and at their faithfulness to God and their church. Their accomplishments have been and continue to be apparent in every field of endeavor from accounting to zoology. And yet, a list of their achievements does not begin to tell the story of their voluntary presence in their church's life and worship, a story of many who share their abilities, expertise, and time with their church and the wider community.

One sign of the Presbyterian Church's gifted membership, a sign shared with other denominations, is the increasing diversity of the Presbyterian Church's leadership, both laity and clergy. More than half of the students in Presbyterian theological seminaries are women. Women serve as pastors of some of the largest Presbyterian congregations, and Presbyterians have grown accustomed to seeing a diversity of lay leaders in monthly communion services.

---

40. John 17:22.

A Vision ... Part One: Seeing the Present

Even the biennial meetings of the Presbyterian Church's General Assembly reflect to some extent an increasing diversity. I first attended a General Assembly in 1970. I would estimate that 95 percent of those who attended that Assembly, both official delegates and visitors, were white; 90 percent were male; and about 60–70 percent were older than 60. Recent General Assemblies have been an obvious contrast to that 1970 Assembly. Racial-ethnic groups and persons, women, and young adults and youth are present in large numbers in today's Assemblies; and they are frequently elected or appointed to Assembly leadership positions. No doubt the Presbyterian Church still has a long way to go before its leadership is truly diverse. Nevertheless, if recent General Assemblies are a sign of the times, Presbyterian Church leadership is more diverse than ever. That diversity is drawing from a rich pool of talented members and at the same time contributing to the life and strength of the Presbyterian Church (U.S.A.).[41]

The presence of gifted members, together with a rich variety of leaders, is cause for thanksgiving among Presbyterians and in any church or denomination that enjoys similar blessings. We should be grateful to God for our members and leaders and pray for them daily. But although they are a reason for thanksgiving, they are not cause for boasting, false pride, or arrogance. Gifted members, with all their talents and their faithfulness, are not a guarantee of future success, well-being, growth, prosperity, or courage. They are a resource, to be sure; but they are not an all-purpose solution to all problems.

At the end of an article on church membership in the twentieth century, church historian Ted A. Campbell commented on the gifted members who are still present after the "mainline decline," the decline in church membership among oldline Protestant denominations, including Presbyterians, from the late 1960s onward:

> So what's left after the fashionable, nominal oldline church members of the mid-20th century fade away? Probably neither the mighty American mainline that never was nor the handful of wrinkled churchgoers

---

41. Williams, "Envisioning the Presbyterian Church (U.S.A.)," 11.

OLD MAN DREAMING

depicted in popular reports. What remains are Christian communities with a stronger core of committed and active believers than is often represented—communities with durable institutions capable of transmitting church cultures across generations.[42]

In a time of anxiety and fracture, Campbell's positive assessment of our church members is noteworthy.

Short-Term and Technically Focused

When I look at the Presbyterian Church (U.S.A.), I see a church that is more often short-term and technically focused than it is long-term and adaptive.

Ronald A. Heifetz, a psychiatrist and senior lecturer at the Harvard Kennedy School of Government, recognized that there are two basic kinds of work: technical and adaptive. Technical work occurs in situations in which the problem definitions are clear and the solutions and implementation are also clear.[43] We know what the problems are and how to respond to them. Such clarity, however, does not mean that technical work is always simple, easy, or unimportant.[44] Surgery to remove a tumor or certain engineering problems in design and construction are technical work and at the same time very complex, difficult, and important.

In contrast to technical work, adaptive work occurs in situations in which both the problem definitions and the solutions are unclear.[45] We do not know what the problems are or how to respond to them. Consequently adaptive work requires learning, and sometimes a large group of people must learn together. Said Heifetz:

> Adaptive work consists of the learning required to address conflicts in the values people hold, or to diminish the gap between the values people stand for and the

---

42. Campbell, "Glory Days?," 13.
43. Heifetz, *Leadership Without Easy Answers*, 76.
44. Ibid., 71–72.
45. Ibid., 76

reality they face. Adaptive work requires a change in values, beliefs, or behavior.[46]

In situations in which the problem definitions are clear but the solutions are unclear, this mixed technical-adaptive work requires learning and should be treated as adaptive.[47]

The distinction between technical and adaptive situations not only applies to work; it also applies to the exercise of leadership and followers' expectations of their leaders. In technical situations a leader defines the problem(s), identifies the solution(s), and answers followers' questions about the problem(s) and solution(s). A leader protects followers from external threats whenever possible, orients followers to their tasks and roles, restores order when conflict arises, and maintains organizational or societal norms.[48] In technical situations a leader should be someone with a certain amount of expertise, a person whose actions and speech are authoritative (but not authoritarian).

Adaptive situations, however, require an altogether different kind of leadership. Heifetz contrasted the two forms of leadership in a single sentence about an adaptive leader:

> Rather than fulfilling the expectation for answers, one provides questions; rather than protecting people from outside threat, one lets people feel the threat in order to stimulate adaptation; instead of orienting people to their current roles, one disorients people so that new role relationships develop; rather than quelling conflict, one generates it; instead of maintaining norms, one challenges them.[49]

Added Heifetz, "Leadership will consist not of answers or assured visions but of taking actions to clarify values."[50]

---

46. Ibid., 22.
47. Ibid., 76.
48. Ibid., 127.
49. Ibid., 126.
50. Ibid., 35.

Heifetz's technical-adaptive dichotomy raises two very practical questions, one about leaders and the other about followers. Can leaders change their form of leadership from technical to adaptive and vice versa? And can followers recognize the need for such a change and adapt accordingly? Heifetz did not claim that either change is impossible, but he did suggest that recognizing the need for such a change might be difficult for both leaders and followers. And he noted that followers might have more difficulty than leaders:

> [I]n a crisis we tend to look for the wrong kind of leadership. We call for someone with answers, decision, strength, and a map of the future, someone who knows where we ought to be going—in short, someone who can make hard problems simple. But problems . . . are not simple. Instead of looking for saviors, we should be calling for leadership that will challenge us to face problems for which there are no simple, painless solutions—problems that require us to learn new ways.[51]

Heifetz's dichotomy is readily applicable to the Presbyterian Church (U.S.A.), much of whose work is in fact short-term and technical. From congregations to national structures, we Presbyterians often know what we must do, what problems we will confront, and how to respond. In congregations such work includes weekly worship preparation; the education of children, youth, and adults; an annual financial campaign; the care of members; local mission initiatives; organizational and denominational obligations; and much more. In regional councils such work involves the health and vitality of congregations; support for and oversight of ministers; mission initiatives needing a wider support base; and a host of plans, programs, administrative tasks, and regulations to enable our work together. At the national level our work is centered on national and global mission concerns, issues of denominational oversight and governance, and programs to benefit the entire Presbyterian Church. These tasks, although technical, are often complex and difficult, and almost always important.

---

51. Ibid., 2.

Fortunately our leaders, both laity and clergy, have the requisite expertise and commitment.

But much of the Presbyterian Church's work is neither short-term nor technical. Earlier I noted the challenges of living in a secular context, of the effects of chronic anxiety among us, and of the fracturing of our body, as well as the strength of gifted members. These are but a few of the challenges and opportunities that are emerging from contemporary cultural, social, economic, or technological changes. We also face crises from theological differences and church divisions, questions about the depth and health of our communal life and our public witness, and the real question of our future as a denomination. These are long-term and adaptive challenges. They touch the Presbyterian Church's deepest sensitivities and involve entrenched, long-term, and systemic difficulties.[52] We don't yet know how to respond to them, but we can be reasonably certain that the tried and true methods by which we have approached short-term and technical situations—organizing and reorganizing; program development; skillful management; use of administrative processes, experts, and expertise; and polity and regulation—won't resolve our long-term, adaptive challenges. Resolution will require us to clarify our beliefs and values and learn some new ways.

When I reflect on my experience as a church executive, and specifically on experiences in planning and visioning, several observations stand out:

- The planning and visioning processes in which I participated resembled processes used in secular organizations.
- Except for a few people who referred to Proverbs 29:18, most of those with whom I worked in planning and visioning never inquired about the Bible's vision stories, its other texts about vision, or what the Bible as a whole could teach us as we plan.
- Christian beliefs, the church's creeds and confessions, and theological reflection and dialogue rarely played a role in planning and visioning processes.

52. Williams, "Thought Provoking," 56.

- The administrative tasks of the church, including planning and visioning, are being conducted without cognizance of different forms of seeing or types of vision such as visual imagination or vision as divine disclosure.
- Although the Presbyterian Church (U.S.A.) pays attention to many aspects of its context, it often overlooks the deeper, more philosophical movements surrounding it.
- Church executives are frequently expected to work and think within short time periods (months, weeks, or days) and seldom expected to work or think in longer time periods (years, decades).
- The adaptive challenges of a secular age, a fracturing body, and our church family's chronic anxiety with its blaming and a quick-fix mentality are as deeply felt among church executives as they are among other groups.

In short, there are adaptive challenges aplenty in the Presbyterian Church (U.S.A.); but I have seen little interest in or support for behaviors that would actually make us more adaptive. To be honest, the majority of my work as a church executive was short-term and technical.

If the Presbyterian Church (U.S.A.) intends to become more adaptive, it will need to rebalance and refocus the work of its committees, agencies, councils, and administrators with increasing emphasis on adaptive behaviors—clarifying beliefs and values, asking questions, listening to diverse perspectives, group learning, imaginative thinking, long term thinking—and decreasing emphasis on technical behaviors—organizing and reorganizing, program development, short-term thinking, experts and expertise, and regulation. Perhaps we should begin by simply telling the truth about the work we are, and are not, doing.

8

A Vision for the Presbyterian Church (U.S.A.)

Part 2: *Visualizing Paths Toward the Future*

ALTHOUGH I CANNOT SEE or know the future with certainty, I can visualize, imagine, and hope for a future. My visions, my dreams, are modest interim steps between the present moment and the future God has in store for us. They are paths or directions that appear promising and challenging and that, if pursued, might strengthen the church for the long haul.

Short-term and technical methods won't solve the Presbyterian Church (U.S.A.)'s most deeply rooted dilemmas or its entrenched, systemic difficulties. Long-term, adaptive approaches are needed; and they are what I am seeking. I can imagine two complementary paths toward the Presbyterian Church's future, paths that are modest, long-term, and promote adaptive learning, as well as two supplementary paths that might strengthen the first two.

Theological Conversation

When I consider paths toward the Presbyterian Church (U.S.A.)'s future, I visualize a church that inspires and promotes frequent theological conversation(s) among its members and leaders.

By "frequent" I mean at least monthly, frequently enough for a group to sustain itself and to provide continuity in its conversation. Groups that meet less frequently inevitably lose momentum and sometimes must reconstitute themselves as a group after too long an absence from one another.

By "theological conversation" I mean conversations about God, God's creation, and God's people. These are immense, diverse, wide-ranging subjects. Theological conversations, therefore, may include, but need not be limited to, discussions of God's nature or traditional church teachings or doctrines. They may encompass a range of topics and disciplines, from the actions of God in the world or in Jesus Christ or through the Holy Spirit, to biblical studies, to the faith and practices of individual Christians, to the life, worship, ministries, and mission of Christian communities. Conversations about interpretations of or contemporary meanings of biblical texts are theological. Conversations about church history and tradition are theological. Simple small group dialogues about what we believe and complex debates on Christian thought in modern culture are both theological. Conversations on issues within Christian ethics are theological. Discussions on the basis for and the practice of a range of church concerns—education, worship, preaching, care of people, stewardship, mission, administration, and many more—are theological. Theological conversation need not be obscure or enigmatic and should not be divorced from all human experience, intelligence, emotion, imagination, or relationships. It should instead be an opportunity to clarify beliefs and values, to ask challenging questions, to experience diverse perspectives, to learn with and from others, and to think creatively about the long term—i.e., an opportunity for adaptive behavior.

So, why should we promote theological conversation? First, it is a means of connecting us to the roots of our faith and ultimately to God who has called us and sustains our faith. As we converse with each other and with biblical texts, we see and hear God's work and voice from the past and discover what God is doing and saying in the present. As we focus together on the person and work of Jesus Christ, we discern who God is; comprehend God's love, justice,

A Vision... Part Two: Visualizing Paths

and truth; understand the extent to which God has acted on our behalf; and recognize who we are and are not. As we study together our history and our traditions, we see how those who preceded us have shaped and continue to shape us. As we discuss together the ethical issues of our day in the light of our faith, the complexity of the issues, our complicity in the world's evil, and our need for divine guidance confront us. And when we pray together for the suffering, the oppressed, the lonely, we remember that God's grace alone is the source of all comfort

A second reason to encourage theological conversation is that every generation of Christians must rearticulate its faith in the idiom of its day and for the people of its time. Philosophies, images, concepts, cultures, art forms, technologies, rhetoric, and worldviews—all shift and change from one generation to the next. The previous generation's theology is never totally adequate for the current generation, and the current generation's theology won't be totally adequate for the next. Ongoing theological conversation is a way of placing previous generations' theologies in conversation with new philosophies, thought forms, and worldviews. What is and what should be the relationship between our past and present theologies and new forms of thought? Which new philosophies and worldviews should we consider as we rearticulate the Christian message, and which ones must we challenge or even oppose? Such questions merit the attention of all church leaders and members, especially in the present secular context in which an exclusive, self-sufficient humanism is contesting most forms of religious belief and practice.

There is a third reason to promote theological conversation: it can enable faithful responses to questions about vision and visioning, about our secular context, and about the present state of the church. Throughout this book I have raised, explicitly or implicitly, questions about vision and visioning. For example, should church organizations borrow management or visioning techniques from secular organizations?[1] What philosophical or theological ideas undergird various organizations and their visions?[2] What do bibli-

---

1. See chapter 1.
2. See chapter 2.

cal texts about vision show us or call us to do?[3] What is imagination's place in church life and theology?[4] Theological conversations provide avenues for wrestling with these and similar questions.

Theological conversations also provide ways to begin responding to our secularized context and to the present state of the Presbyterian Church (U.S.A.). I say "begin responding" because these conversations are only necessary first steps in longer processes of responding. To respond to our secular age, we must first clarify our own beliefs and values and differentiate ourselves from the exclusive, self-sufficient humanism surrounding us. To respond to the chronic anxiety within the Presbyterian Church, we must first define who we are and what we stand for. To appreciate our gifted members, we need first to see them as God's people, not merely as a pool of volunteer labor. To refocus the Presbyterian Church's time and energy on adaptive behaviors, we need first to identify our convictions and principles. Theological conversations are starting points for long-term responses to our most difficult and most deeply rooted dilemmas, and the Presbyterian Church's *Book of Confessions* is a primary resource for these conversations.

There is a fourth reason to promote theological conversation: it can reveal God's criticism, God's judgment on Christians and the church.[5] In 1939 at the end of his second and last visit to the United States, Dietrich Bonhoeffer wrote his observations of American Christians and the American church. He titled his observations "Protestantism without Reformation." Here are some sentences from its final paragraph:

> God has granted American Christianity no Reformation. He has given it strong revivalist preachers, churchmen and theologians, but no Reformation of the church of Jesus Christ by the Word of God.... American theology and the American church as a whole have never been able to understand the meaning of "criticism" by the Word of

---

3. See chapters 4 and 5.

4. See chapter 6.

5. Re: the concept "God's criticism" and Bonhoeffer's critique of American Christianity, see McBride, *Church for the World*, 38.

A Vision... Part Two: Visualizing Paths

God and all that signifies. Right to the last they do not understand that God's "criticism" touches even religion, the Christianity of the churches and the sanctification of Christians, and that God has founded his church beyond religion and beyond ethics.[6]

A key phrase in this paragraph is "'criticism' by the Word of God." Bonhoeffer was saying to both Germans and Americans that the Word of God in Jesus Christ is the one and only foundation for any critical examination of or critical judgment about Christianity or the church. Theological conversation, especially around God's Word, can uncover for us God's critique of our faith and life together. Although it may be temporarily painful, we need this critique for the maturation of our Christian faith and life.

When we consider the number of groups that already exist in Protestant congregations, opportunities for frequent theological conversation abound and await implementation. Many ministers, for example, participate in lectionary study groups, groups that already engage in theological conversation. Congregations with staffs usually have regular staff meetings. Creative leadership by heads of staff can transform parts of these meetings into theological conversations. The councils that oversee a congregation's life and ministry (known as sessions in Presbyterian churches) often meet monthly and are a most appropriate setting for theological conversation among pastors and lay leadership. And carefully selected readings or well-framed questions might be enough to begin theological conversation in committee meetings, prayer groups, or even choir practices.

Although opportunities for frequent theological conversation are abundant in congregations, they are not always as plentiful among judicatory and national church leaders. We expect our district, regional, and national leaders to perform a multitude of technical tasks, tasks that leave little time for ongoing theological conversation or for most adaptive behaviors. What if the Presbyterian Church (U.S.A.) actually altered its expectations of its executive leaders? What if it revised their job descriptions to reduce

---

6. Bonhoeffer, "Protestantism without Reformation," 117.

their technical tasks and to encourage participation in theological conversations and forms of adaptive work? What if our executives really had the time and the incentive to join neighboring pastors in a lectionary study group? These and similar changes will be essential if the Presbyterian Church expects its executives to provide leadership for a church that inspires and promotes frequent theological conversation(s).

Although most Presbyterians do not realize it, the idea of promoting theological conversation(s) is an old idea in the Reformed tradition. It goes back to sixteenth-century Geneva's Venerable Company of Pastors.[7] The first mention of the Venerable Company appears in these paragraphs on the office of pastor in John Calvin's 1541 "Draft Ecclesiastical Ordinances":

> First it will be expedient that all the ministers, for conserving purity and concord of doctrine among themselves, meet together one certain day each week, for discussion of the Scriptures.
>
> If there appear differences of doctrine, let the ministers come together to discuss the matter. Afterwards, if need be, let them call the elders to assist in composing the contention.
>
> To obviate all scandals of living, it will be proper that there be a form of correction to which all submit themselves. It will also be the means by which the ministry may retain respect, and the Word of God be neither dishonoured nor scorned.[8]

Calvin was attempting to reform the Genevan church in accord with Reformation theology, but without returning to medieval enchantment or Catholic hierarchy. Theologian Joseph Small assessed the results of Calvin's reformation and offered some wisdom to the contemporary church:

> Geneva's Venerable Company of Pastors recorded its roster and the proceedings of its meetings in *The Register of the*

---

7. For calling this to my attention, I am indebted to Small, "Travail of the Presbytery," 58–61.

8. Calvin, "Draft Ecclesiastical Ordinances," 60.

A Vision . . . Part Two: Visualizing Paths

Company Pastors. These sixteenth century records reveal a gathering of pastors who placed Scripture and worship, theology and prayer, at the center of the church's life and the heart of pastoral vocation. *In an age of ecclesial uncertainty and pastoral confusion, the pattern is suggestive.*[9]

Leadership

When I reflect upon paths toward the Presbyterian Church (U.S.A.)'s future, I visualize a church that encourages and challenges its ordered ministers to faithful, mature, resilient, courageous, and imaginative leadership.

"Ordered ministers" is the official name of those who have been called and ordained to one of three ordered ministries (formerly called offices) in the Presbyterian Church (U.S.A.). The three ordered ministries are deacon, ruling elder, and minister of the Word and Sacrament (also called teaching elder). Their respective functions are the ministry of compassion and service, the ministry of discernment and governance, and the ministry of the Word and Sacrament.[10] The ordered ministers are not only the Presbyterian Church's official leaders. They are in most circumstances its real leaders, and they clearly hold most of its leadership positions and responsibilities.

By envisioning the Presbyterian Church as encouraging and challenging its ordered ministers to leadership, I am not recommending changes in Presbyterian polity or in the qualifications and responsibilities of the Presbyterian Church's ordered ministries. Presbyterian polity is adequate for defining, calling, and preparing ordered ministers; and Presbyterians have recognized leadership gifts in those whom they have called to ordered ministries. I am instead recommending that the Presbyterian Church nourish and develop leaders' innate and acquired gifts and that it challenge them to grow spiritually, mentally, and emotionally.

9. Small, "Travail of the Presbytery," 60 (emphasis added).

10. *Constitution of the Presbyterian Church (U.S.A.)*, G-2.0102, G-2.0201, G-2.0301, G-2.0501, 25–27 and 29.

But why should the Presbyterian Church pay so much attention to its leadership? Why is leadership so important in and for this church? Because its leaders, through word or deed or both, are a primary link between God's good news, as revealed in Jesus Christ, the Bible, and the faith of the church, and the people of God, both those in the church and the rest of humankind. Deacons make the connection between God's good news and God's people through their service and compassion. Ruling elders make this connection with their discernment and governance. Ministers make it by teaching, preaching, and administration of sacraments. These leaders, because of their positions, will influence what the church says and does in the present and what it will say and do in the future. The Presbyterian Church and its congregations draw a great deal of strength from the strength of its leaders; and its leaders set the tone for an enormous share of the church's work and witness, both within the church and in the surrounding world.

In the early decades of my ministry, books and articles on leadership occasionally came to my attention. Most of those works, however, did not apply to churches or religious organizations; and most, in my opinion, did not adequately account for critical aspects of leadership that I had observed and experienced.

Around 1990 a close friend and colleague recommended that I read a book by a rabbi and therapist, Ed Friedman. I eventually bought the book and began reading. In a chapter titled "Leadership and Self in a Congregational Family," I read the following:

> The basic concept of leadership through self-differentiation is this: If a leader will take primary responsibility for his or her own position as "head" and work to define his or her own goals and self, while *staying in touch* with the rest of the organism, there is a more than reasonable chance that the body will follow.
>
> This emphasis on a leader's self-differentiation is not to be confused with *independence* or some kind of selfish individuality. On the contrary, we are talking about the ability of a leader to be a self while still remaining a part of the system. It is the most difficult thing in the world in any family.

A Vision . . . Part Two: Visualizing Paths

> There are three distinct but interrelated components to leadership through self-differentiation. . . . First and foremost, the leader must stay in touch.
>
> The second central component is the capacity and willingness of the leader to take nonreactive, clearly conceived, and clearly defined positions.
>
> The third component in a family systems approach to leadership [is] the capacity to deal with the sabotage.[11]

As soon as I had read these sentences, I realized that I had seen for the first time in my life a reasonably clear and concise definition of leadership. Friedman, by understanding leadership as an emotional process in an emotional field, had captured in a few paragraphs the major components of leadership: its relational character, the specific tasks of the leader, and its complexity and difficulty. Furthermore, his definition of leadership was and is universally applicable to any system regardless of size, including churches and other religious organizations.

After his initial statements on leadership through self-differentiation, Friedman actively sought to deepen his own understanding of the concept.[12] He began writing a book on leadership, but his death in 1996 brought his work to an abrupt halt. Family and friends published his unfinished manuscripts; and former colleagues and students continue to study, discuss, and apply his concept of leadership through self-differentiation and other concepts in emotional process.[13] Meanwhile other people and concepts have contributed to our understanding of leadership, such as Ronald Heifetz's concept of technical and adaptive work requiring different kinds of leadership. Today the subject of leadership is a clearer, more thoroughly defined topic than it was when my ministry began.

So, what kind of leadership does the church need? I believe the Presbyterian Church should encourage and challenge its

---

11. Friedman, *Generation to Generation*, 229–30.

12. For Friedman's later thoughts on leadership through self-differentiation, see Friedman, *Failure of Nerve*, 183–86, 229–47.

13. For an example of a restatement and application of Friedman's thought, see Duggan and Moyer, *Resilient Leadership*.

ordered ministers to faithful, mature, resilient, courageous, and imaginative leadership.

The church needs faithful leaders, leaders faithful to the triune God, to Jesus Christ, to the gospel, and to theological and ethical principles. From these basic commitments, other kinds of faithfulness emerge, such as staying in touch with congregants, constituents, and other leaders; keeping one's ordination vows; and even keeping everyday promises to return phone calls, answer emails, and keep appointments. Leaders are faithful to their vocational tasks; they focus their time, energy, and thought on the work to which they are called. They take stands against fracture and polarization. They lead with helpful technical and adaptive behaviors: expertise, clarifying beliefs and values, asking questions, openness to diverse perspectives, commitment to group learning, long-term and imaginative thinking. And when they remain in touch with congregants and constituents, anxious congregations and church councils tend to remain faithful to the whole church. The faithfulness of leadership is a countercultural witness to our God, who was and is faithful to us in Jesus Christ and who remains faithful to us through the Holy Spirit.

The church needs mature leaders. Maturity is not about one's chronological age. It's about the quality of our relationships with other people. There are three components to a leader's maturity: staying in touch with followers, self-definition, and self-regulation. A leader stays in touch with followers, or at least tries to, even when there is disagreement or enmity between them. Staying in touch, therefore, is not as easy as it sounds and may require a degree of creativity from the leader. Self-definition is part of what Friedman meant when he defined "differentiation."[14] It includes "the capacity to take a stand in an intense emotional system, . . . saying 'I' when others are demanding 'we', . . . and being clear about one's own personal values and goals."[15] Self-regulation is the other part of Friedman's definition of differentiation. It includes "containing one's reactivity to the reactivity of others, . . . maintaining a

---

14. Friedman, *Failure of Nerve*, 183.
15. Ibid.

non-anxious presence in the face of anxious others, . . . and taking maximum responsibility for one's own emotional being and destiny rather than blaming others or the context."[16]

Mature leaders know that linking beliefs and values with long-term, adaptive actions takes time and that patience really is a virtue in many circumstances. They understand and use all three forms of seeing or types of vision and all three time perspectives. They define and regulate themselves vis-à-vis the overreactions, herding, blaming, and quick fixes of others. They stand for unity and inclusion rather than fracture and polarization. They acknowledge and work with the gifts, talents, and insights of others. Mature leaders appreciate and perform both technical and adaptive work. Although no one will ever perfectly master the three components of leaders' maturity, leaders can raise their level of maturity and their leadership effectiveness with the help of coaching on any one of the components.

The church needs resilient leaders who can weather the turbulence, conflict, sabotage, and personal criticism surrounding them. Interestingly, the components of resilience are the same as the components of maturity: staying in touch with followers, self-definition, and self-regulation. Mature, resilient leaders listen to and are attuned to followers. They behave with clarity of thought and vision; and they keep their emotions sufficiently in check to be a non-defensive, non-intrusive and non-anxious presence. As we've noted, with a little coaching leaders can raise their level of resilience and their leadership effectiveness.

The church needs courageous leaders who will speak of God and God's love for all in a secular age in which exclusive humanism flourishes. Such leaders remain calm and take principled and well-reasoned stands in the face of overreactions, blaming, and demands for quick fixes. They oppose fracturing and polarization and have the courage to include diverse perspectives in deliberations and to balance technical expertise with adaptive actions. Courageous leaders are not afraid to speak truth to power, to challenge falsehoods and divisive rhetoric, and to express themselves honestly without exaggeration.

16. Ibid.

The church needs leaders who can imagine a rebalancing of the church's work to make it more adaptive; who can visualize a greater role for the laity in the church's life; who can envisage a richer, healthier unity and inclusion among its members; and who can see new forms of witness to and new relationships with a secularized culture. Through imaginative leaders, with lots of help from the Holy Spirit, ancient vision stories and other texts about vision can speak anew; and multiple forms of seeing can thrive among God's people. Creative congregations and church organizations almost always have imaginative leadership.

As the Presbyterian Church (U.S.A.) journeys into an uncertain future, it should not only clarify its beliefs and values—hence, the need for theological conversation—it should also encourage and challenge its ordered ministers to faithful, mature, resilient, courageous, imaginative leadership. These two paths complement each other and will strengthen the Presbyterian Church for the long haul ahead.

Communities of Faithful Practice

When I contemplate paths toward the Presbyterian Church (U.S.A.)'s future, I visualize communities of faithful practice, one of two supplementary paths that might strengthen theological conversation and leadership.

In 2004–2005 Presbyterian theologian John P. Burgess and his family spent a sabbatical year in St. Petersburg, Russia. The Burgess family wanted "to spend a year abroad with Christians whose way of worshipping [they] knew to be profoundly different from [their] own."[17] Burgess' book *Encounters with Orthodoxy* tells the story of their experiences among the Russian Orthodox faithful, experiences that became for them a spiritual journey as much as a physical journey to St. Petersburg. His book introduces North American Protestants to Russian Orthodox worship and practices that many Protestants would consider quite strange; and it creates a dialogue

---

17. Burgess, *Encounters with Orthodoxy*, xiv.

between the Protestant Reformers who critiqued the practices of late medieval Catholicism and contemporary Orthodox theologians who provide the rationale for Orthodoxy's practices.

His book also lets Orthodoxy and North American Protestantism speak to, learn from, and even criticize each other. Through chapters on Orthodox concepts of holiness, ritual, beauty, miracles, monasticism, the Eucharist, and the church, Burgess contrasts Orthodoxy with Protestantism and identifies what he believes Orthodoxy can teach Protestants. On the subject of holiness, for example, he says, "For the Orthodox the story of the transfiguration is at the heart of the gospel. . . . The Orthodox believe that our purpose is to grow into this vision of God's holiness."[18] They understand churches to be holy places, and they expect the liturgy to lead them closer to God. In contrast Burgess opines of Protestant worship, "The sense of standing before a holy God has been lost."[19] And of both the Christian faith and the church, Burgess wrote:

> Orthodoxy challenges Protestants not to reduce Christian faith to abstract intellectual doctrines or righteous moral causes. The Orthodox ask us to see God in our midst in a church that is one holy catholic and apostolic—a church that God sustains as a concrete, visible institution on earth, not just as a lofty ideal or invisible reality.[20]

According to Burgess, Orthodoxy's most significant challenge to Protestantism comes from its emphasis on religious practice. Burgess' words speak for themselves:

> As essential as education in the Scriptures and church tradition is, it cannot replace daily practices and disciplines of living the faith. We learn the faith not primarily out of books, lectures, or sermons but by doing with our bodies what the church body does. In religious matters, imitation of physical movements is often the mother of wisdom.

18. Ibid., 21–22.
19. Ibid., 186.
20. Ibid., 182.

> Too many Protestants think that they cannot practice the faith until they understand it. They cannot pray until they understand what prayer is all about, or they cannot say the creed until they have studied it and determined whether they agree with it. The Orthodox look at faith from the opposite angle. One cannot understand prayer until one prays. One cannot reflect on the meaning of the creed until one actually says it.[21]

Although we Protestants can learn from Orthodoxy, we do not have to become Orthodox in order to practice our faith. In fact, we already have the necessary traditions and resources to become communities of faithful practice, if only we would recognize what we have. Scripture, for example, repeatedly points us to God and is a powerful witness to all worshippers when used in liturgy. Our less elaborate forms of the visual arts can focus us on the signs of God's holiness in pulpit, font, and table without resorting to Orthodoxy's ornate forms of beauty. Well-chosen music can remind us of God's love, presence, and justice at an emotional depth that words cannot touch. Prayer, starting with the Lord's Prayer, and practices of prayer can be taught to almost any age, from young children to the oldest adult. We have long recognized that we need to prepare children to receive their first Communion. What if we also prepared adults for their ongoing experiences at the Lord's Table? John Calvin recognized that a holy life required the mutual encouragement and accountability of a community. For Calvin that community was not a monastery, but a congregation or a family. How can we reinvigorate our congregations and families as places of holiness?[22] How can we recognize our service to the poor and needy, our service in our communities, or our vocations as parts of God's call to a holy life? What would it mean for a Presbyterian to go on a pilgrimage instead of taking a vacation or even a "mission trip"?

Not every congregation will become a community of faithful practice; but those whose pastors and people have a more than average interest in worship, prayer, spiritual disciplines, visual arts,

21. Ibid., 189–90.
22. Ibid., 132–33.

or music are good candidates for becoming such a community. Such communities will teach and encourage their members to participate actively in worship and to pray daily and imaginatively. They will engage members' whole being, body, mind, and spirit; and eventually they will offer more than a superficial knowledge of the Bible and Christian beliefs, more than passive participation in a one-hour-per-week worship service. Communities of faithful practice will be a helpful addition to future theological conversations. In such communities, practices and theological conversations will reinforce each other and offer a multidimensional approach to Christian faith and witness.

Crossing Boundaries

When I think about paths toward the Presbyterian Church (U.S.A.)'s future, I visualize Christians, congregations, and a whole church that crosses cultural, social, economic, racial, and political boundaries in the name of Jesus Christ. This is the second supplementary path that might strengthen the Presbyterian Church.

Through what I would describe as imaginatively seeing the past, missiologist Andrew Walls surveyed twenty centuries of Christian history for generalizations about the transmission of the faith worldwide. He identified three generalizations. The first "is that Christian advance is not progressive, but serial."[23] Walls explained:

> Christian advance is not a progressive process, a steady line of success. Advance may not produce further advance, but recession. . . . Christian advance is serial, rooted first in one place and then in another, decaying in one area, appearing in another. It would seem that there is a vulnerability at the heart of Christian faith; and indeed the Cross stands a reminder of that vulnerability.[24]

---

23. Walls, "Christianity Across Twenty Centuries," 48.
24. Ibid., 48.

Old Man Dreaming

Walls illustrated the serial nature of Christian advance by citing the recession, because of persecution, of the Jerusalem church[25] and the subsequent mission to the Greco-Roman world. He also noted the twentieth-century decline of Christianity in the West, especially in Western Europe, and the simultaneous rise of Christianity in Africa, Asia, and Latin America.

Walls' second generalization "is that Christianity lives by crossing cultural frontiers."[26] The Christianity of the Jerusalem church might not have survived but for the fact that it had already crossed a cultural boundary into the Greco-Roman world. And Walls said of contemporary Christianity, "That Christianity is not in decline in the world as a whole is due to one simple fact, that . . . the gospel has been crossing cultural frontiers, in Africa and Asia, in the Americas and the Pacific."[27] Walls summarized, "In each case a threatened eclipse of Christianity was averted by its cross-cultural diffusion. Crossing cultural boundaries has been the life blood of historic Christianity."[28]

Walls' third generalization "is that transmission of the faith involves translation, and translation leads to theological expansion."[29] Translation, for Walls, is more than a language problem, more than matching grammatical constructs or words with the same or similar meanings in two different languages. "The message about Christ has to penetrate beyond language . . . ," he said. "It has to pass into the local systems of thinking and choosing, the networks of relationships, that make up identity."[30] Once the process of translation has penetrated a culture's ways of thinking, choosing, and relating, new theological tasks and questions emerge. Walls noted that the doctrines of Trinity and incarnation, as expressed in the church's historic creeds, were the result of theological questions that arose in the translation and penetration of

---

25. Acts 8, 11–12.
26. Walls, "Christianity Across Twenty Centuries," 48.
27. Ibid., 49.
28. Walls, *Cross-Cultural Process in Christian History*, 32.
29. Walls, "Christianity Across Twenty Centuries," 49.
30. Ibid.

Christianity into Greco-Roman culture. He also believed that a similar theological expansion was underway at the beginning of the twenty-first century. "This time," he said, "the field of interaction will be with the cultures of Africa and Asia."[31]

While Walls' generalizations are instructive, the Presbyterian Church (U.S.A.) has its own history of effective cross-cultural mission. In the nineteenth and twentieth centuries we Presbyterians sent missionaries to a multitude of countries and cultures. Our missionaries learned how to cross the boundaries between North American culture and those to whom they were sent. Although missionaries sometimes failed to differentiate between the gospel and Western imperialism, they planted and cultivated the gospel in places and among people very different from us. There the gospel flourished, but not always according to Western patterns. Thanks to our missionaries, globalization is part of our rich mission heritage, not a strategy for economic gain. Thanks to them, we have access to real-world experiences in crossing cultural boundaries.[32]

Walls' generalizations from history and our own history of cross-cultural mission point us toward some possible futures in mission. Walls generalized on a global scale. Suppose we took the contents of his generalizations and applied them on a different scale, a smaller scale such as a district or area, a local community, or a congregation. On a smaller scale we probably won't be crossing oceans or international boundaries, but we will still have boundaries to cross. Such boundaries might include those between the dominant majority and ethnic minorities; between the affluent and the poor; between the well educated and the educationally impoverished; between the powerful and the disenfranchised; between those who practice faith and the so-called "nones"; or among people of different ages, races, social classes, neighborhoods, or ideologies. And when we cross such boundaries, we will still have to translate our message, if not into a different language, at least into the cultural ways of thinking, acting, and relating found in the places we go and among people we meet.

31. Ibid.
32. Williams, "Envisioning the Presbyterian Church (U.S.A.)," 11.

Old Man Dreaming

We have plenty of boundaries to cross in our local communities, and opportunities for transmitting the faith surround us. Those most likely to choose the path of boundary crossing are congregations, church councils, or church members who are already interested in mission or evangelism. I applaud their interest, but I also offer some words of caution. Do not underestimate the strength of our secularized context. Recognize that boundary crossing has deeply theological roots—e.g., God's breaking into human experience in Jesus Christ—and therefore requires ongoing theological conversation. Boundary crossing will need faithful, mature, resilient, courageous, imaginative leadership. And it will require stamina for the road ahead.

Epilogue

Questions at a Threshold

HAVING RECEIVED THE FINDINGS from a churchwide listening effort that the Presbyterian Church's Committee on the Office of the General Assembly conducted in 2015, titled "When We Gather at the Table: A PC(USA) Snapshot,"[1] the 2016 General Assembly of the Presbyterian Church (U.S.A.) voted by a large majority to:

> Name a "2020 Vision Team" of fifteen people to develop a guiding statement for the denomination and make a plan for its implementation with all deliberate speed. The process of developing such a guiding statement will help us to name and claim our denominational identity as we seek to follow the Spirit into the future.[2]

As I write these words, the 2020 Vision Team has been selected; and we Presbyterians are at the threshold of a visioning process.

I, based on my studies of vision and visioning processes, have a list of questions about what to expect in days to come, starting with a question about vision and Scripture. The Bible includes significant stories and other texts about vision. Will the Presbyterian Church, its leaders and members, led by the 2020 Vision Team, study these stories and texts as part of the visioning process? Will the Presbyterian Church pay attention to its biblical resources?

1. *Minutes, 222nd General Assembly, 2016,* 259–78.
2. Ibid., 40, 257–58.

EPILOGUE

Theologically the subject of vision touches aspects of creation, anthropology, the nature of God, revelation, Christology, and ecclesiology; and the opening pages of the Presbyterian *Book of Order* include a vision statement.[3] Will the Presbyterian Church, led by the 2020 Vision Team, study and incorporate insights from Reformed theology and Presbyterian polity into its visioning process?

Imagination is now a category in theological studies, and ordered ministers in the Presbyterian Church vow when ordained to serve with imagination.[4] Will Presbyterians, as part of the visioning process, look to the future with imagination?

American Christians live in a secular age. Will the 2020 Vision Team weigh the philosophical and religious milieu in which the Presbyterian Church now lives and works, and will it invite the Church to ponder this concern with it as part of the visioning process? Will the Presbyterian Church look beyond demographic data and peer deeply into its secularized context?

The Presbyterian Church, its councils, its congregations, its leaders, and its members, all too frequently display symptoms that anxious families display: reactivity, herding, blaming, a quick-fix mentality, and a lack of well-differentiated leadership. Will the Presbyterian Church, led by the 2020 Vision Team, identify and confront honestly, within the visioning process, its symptoms of and faithful responses to its own anxieties?

"When We Gather at the Table" identified four "segments," clusters of Presbyterians who share particular values distinct from other clusters of Presbyterians. Based on my experience in the Presbyterian Church, I surmise that in each segment there are God-given strengths and abilities that are unique to that segment and that the Presbyterian Church needs. I also surmise that discovery of those strengths and abilities might be a partial antidote to the fracturing of our church body. Will the 2020 Vision Team seek to discover the unique strengths and abilities of all the Church's segments; and will it engage the Presbyterian Church, through the visioning process, in its discovery?

3. *Constitution of the Presbyterian Church (U.S.A.)*, F-1.0301, 2.
4. Ibid., W-4.4003, 123.

Questions at a Threshold

I am convinced that the Presbyterian Church needs an increased emphasis on adaptive work: clarifying beliefs and values, asking questions, incorporating diverse perspectives, encouraging group learning, and thinking imaginatively about the long term. Will the Presbyterian Church's councils and congregations, through the visioning process and beyond, redirect at least some of their time and energy to adaptive work?

As the Presbyterian Church visualizes its future, will it, beginning with the 2020 Vision Team, inspire and promote frequent theological conversations among its councils, congregations, leaders, and members? Will it encourage and challenge its ordered ministers to faithful, mature, resilient, courageous, and imaginative leadership? Will it develop and nurture communities of faithful practice? Will it inspire boundary-crossing mission in our communities and the world? In other words, will the Presbyterian Church (U.S.A.) pursue paths that will strengthen the church and its witness for the long term? I hope the answers are "Yes" to all of these questions, starting with my question about vision and Scripture.

If the Presbyterian Church bypasses or merely scratches the surface of one or more of these questions, I fear that this latest visioning process will end as late-twentieth- and early-twenty-first-century processes in secular and church organizations ended: inadequate, powerless, captive to organizational self-interests, and buried in a digital file in an unknown computer. I, as an old man, am dreaming of something better for my church.

Glory be to the God of seeing, who is seen in Jesus Christ.[5] Amen.

---

5. Gen 16:13; John 1:14, 18; 9:35–39.

Bibliography

Abbott-Smith, George. *A Manual Greek Lexicon of the New Testament*. 3rd ed. New York: Scribner's, 1936.
Barna, George. *The Power of Vision*. Ventura, CA: Regal, 2003.
Barrett, C. K. *The Gospel According to St. John: An Introduction with Commentary and Notes on the Greek Text*. London: SPCK, 1962.
Bauer, Walter, Frederick W. Danker, W. F. Arndt, and F. W. Gingrich. *A Greek-English Lexicon of the New Testament and Other Early Christian Literature*. Chicago: University of Chicago Press, 1957.
Blount, Brian K. *Revelation: A Commentary*. New Testament Library. Louisville: Westminster John Knox, 2009.
Bonhoeffer, Dietrich. "Protestantism without Reformation." In *No Rusty Swords: Letters, Lectures, and Notes, 1929–1936, from the Collected Works of Dietrich Bonhoeffer*, edited by Edwin H. Robertson, 92–118. New York: Harper and Row, 1965.
Bornkamm, Gunther. *Jesus of Nazareth*. Translated by Irene McLuskey, Fraser McLuskey, and James M. Robinson. New York: Harper and Row, 1960.
Brown, Francis, S. R. Driver, and Charles A. Briggs. *A Hebrew and English Lexicon of the Old Testament*. Oxford: Clarendon, 1907.
Brueggemann, Walter. *An Introduction to the Old Testament: The Canon and Christian Imagination*. Louisville: Westminster John Knox, 2003.
———. *Mandate to Difference: An Invitation to the Contemporary Church*. Louisville: Westminster John Knox, 2007.
Bryant, David J. *Faith and the Play of Imagination: On the Role of Imagination in Religion*. Studies in American Biblical Hermeneutics 5. Macon, GA: Mercer University Press, 1989.
Burgess, John P. *Encounters with Orthodoxy: How Protestant Churches Can Reform Themselves Again*. Louisville: Westminster John Knox, 2013.

Bibliography

Calvin, John. "Draft Ecclesiastical Ordinances, September and October 1541." In *Calvin; Theological Treatises*, edited and translated by J. K. S. Reid, 58–72. Louisville: Westminster John Knox, 2006.

Campbell, Ted A. "Glory Days?: The Myth of the Mainline." *The Christian Century*, 9 July 2014, 11–13.

Carter, Rita. *Mapping the Mind*. Berkeley: University of California Press, 1999.

Cohn, Nate. "Polarization Is Dividing American Society, Not Just Politics." *New York Times*, online edition, 12 July 2014. https://www.nytimes.com/2014/06/12/upshot/polarization-is-dividing-american-society-not-just-politics.html.

The Constitution of the Presbyterian Church (U.S.A.): Part II, Book of Order 2015–17. Louisville: Office of the General Assembly, 2011.

Duggan, Robert, and James Moyer. *Resilient Leadership: Navigating the Hidden Chemistry of Organizations*. West Conshohocken, PA: Infinity, 2009.

Eissfeldt, Otto. *The Old Testament: An Introduction, Including the Apocrypha and Pseudegrapha, and Also the Works of Similar Type from Qumran: The History of the Formation of the Old Testament*. Translated by Peter R. Ackroyd. New York: Harper and Row, 1965.

Feine, Paul, and Johannes Behm. *Introduction to the New Testament*. 14th rev. ed. Edited by Werner Georg Kummel, translated by A. J. Mattill Jr. Nashville: Abington, 1966.

Friedman, Edwin H. *A Failure of Nerve: Leadership in the Age of the Quick Fix*. Edited by Margaret M. Treadwell and Edward W. Beal. New York: Seabury/Church Publishing, 2007.

———. *Generation to Generation: Family Process in Church and Synagogue*. New York: Guilford, 1985.

Guthrie, Shirley C. *Christian Doctrine*. Rev. ed. Louisville: Westminster John Knox, 1994.

Heifetz, Ronald A. *Leadership Without Easy Answers*. Cambridge, MA: Belknap Press of Harvard University Press, 1994.

Jepsen, Alfred. "Chazah." In *Theological Dictionary of the Old Testament*, edited by G. Johannes Botterweck and Helmer Ringgren, translated by Geoffrey W. Bromiley et al., 4:280–90. Grand Rapids: Eerdmans, 1980.

Jinkins, Michael. *The Church Faces Death: Ecclesiology in a Post-Modern Context*. New York: Oxford University Press, 1999.

Kerr, Michael E., and Murray Bowen. *Family Evaluation: An Approach Based on Bowen Theory*. New York: Norton, 1988.

Koehler, Ludwig, and Walter Baumgartner, eds. *Lexicon in Veteris Testamenti Libros*. Leiden: Brill, 1958.

Kotter, John P. *Leading Change*. Boston: Harvard Business Review Press, 1996.

Maitland, Sara. *A Big-Enough God: Artful Theology*. London: Mowbrey, 1995.

Mancini, Will. *Church Unique: How Missional Leaders Cast Vision, Capture Culture, and Create Movement*. San Francisco: Jossey-Bass, 2008.

McBride, Jennifer M. *The Church for the World: A Theology of Public Witness*. New York: Oxford University Press, 2012.

Bibliography

Minutes, 222nd General Assembly, 2016: Part I, Journal. Louisville: Office of the General Assembly, 2016.

Muilenburg, James. *The Way of Israel: Biblical Faith and Ethics*. Religious Perspectives 5. New York: Harper & Bros., 1961.

Munck, Johannes. *Paul and the Salvation of Mankind*. Richmond: John Knox, 1959.

Nanus, Burt. *Visionary Leadership: Creating a Compelling Sense of Direction for Your Organization*. San Francisco: Jossey-Bass, 1992.

Park, Suzie. "Story, Interpretation, and Identity." *Insights: The Faculty Journal of Austin Seminary* 129.1 (Fall 2013) 3–10.

Rad, Gerhard von. *Old Testament Theology*. Vol. 2: *The Theology of Israel's Prophetic Traditions*. Translated by D. M. G. Stalker. New York: Harper & Row, 1965.

The Random House Dictionary of the English Language. Edited by Jess Stein, Laurence Urdang, et al. New York: Random House, 1971.

Rodgers, Daniel T. *Age of Fracture*. Cambridge, MA: Belknap Press of Harvard University Press, 2011.

Senge, Peter M. *The Fifth Discipline: The Art and Practice of the Learning Organization*. New York: Doubleday/Currency, 1990.

Small, Joseph D. "The Travail of the Presbytery." In *A Collegial Bishop?: Classis and Presbytery at Issue*, edited by Allen J Janssen and Leon van den Brocke, 47–61. Grand Rapids: Eerdmans, 2010.

Smith, James K. A. *How (Not) to Be Secular: Reading Charles Taylor*. Grand Rapids: Eerdmans, 2014.

Smith, Ted A. Review of *How (Not) to Be Secular: Reading Charles Taylor* by James K. A. Smith. *The Christian Century*, 24 June 2015, 42.

Stacey, Ralph D. *Managing the Unknowable: Strategic Boundaries Between Order and Chaos in Organizations*. San Francisco: Jossey-Bass, 1992.

Swan, Sandra S. *The New Outreach: Doing Good the Better Way: An ABC Planning Guide*. New York: Church Publishing, 2010.

Taylor, Charles. *A Secular Age*. Cambridge, MA: Belknap Press of Harvard University Press, 2007.

Viereck, George Sylvester. "What Life Means to Einstein: An Interview by George Sylvester Viereck." *Saturday Evening Post*, 26 October 1929, 117.

Walls, Andrew F. "Christianity Across Twenty Centuries." In *Atlas of Global Christianity 1910–2010*, edited by Todd M. Johnson and Kenneth R. Ross, 48–49. Edinburgh: Edinburgh University Press, 2009.

———. *The Cross-Cultural Process in Christian History: Studies in the Transmission and Appropriation of Faith*. Maryknoll, NY: Orbis, 2002.

Warnock, Mary. *Imagination*. London: Faber & Faber, 1976.

Webster's Ninth New Collegiate Dictionary. Edited by Frederick C. Mish. Springfield, MA: Merriam-Webster, 1986.

Webster's Third New International Dictionary of the English Language Unabridged. Edited by Philip Babcock Gove. Springfield, MA: G. & C. Merriam, 1961.

Bibliography

Wilder, Amos Niven. *Theopoetic: Theology and the Religious Imagination*. Lima, OH: Academic Renewal, 2001.

Williams, John L. "Envisioning the Presbyterian Church (U.S.A.)." *The Presbyterian Outlook* 188.26 (July 31/August 7, 2006) 10–15, 20.

———. "Thought Provoking, but Insufficient: A Reply to William J. Weston's 'Rebuilding the Presbyterian Establishment.'" In *Beyond Rebuilding?: Shaping a Life Together*, 54–59. Re-Forming Ministry Occasional Paper 4. Louisville: Presbyterian Church (U.S.A.), 2009.

Wilson, Robert R. *Prophecy and Society in Ancient Israel*. Philadelphia: Fortress, 1980.

Wolin, Sheldon S. *Politics and Vision: Continuity and Innovation in Western Political Thought*. Princeton, NJ: Princeton University Press, 2004.

Yoder, Christine Roy. "On the Threshold of Kingship: A Study of Agur (Proverbs 30)." *Interpretation* 63.3 (July 2009) 254–63.

Index

Acute anxiety, 110–12
Adaptive leadership, 119–20
Adaptive work, 118–19, 121
Angelophanies, 28, 33
Anxious family, 110–13
Apocalyptic literature, 28, 33–34
Auditions, 27–28, 31–32, 47–50

Barna, George, 1, 10–13, 15, 18, 20, 39–40, 44
Bible's earlier vision stories, 22–34
    challenge contemporary concepts of vision, 35
    characteristics, 23
    direct and unmediated, 32
    specific, distinct, identifiable, 28–32
    vocabulary of seeing, 23–28, 23n1, 35
Blount, Brian, 34
Bonhoeffer, Dietrich, 127–28
Bornkamm, Gunther, 66–67
Brueggemann, Walter, 59–60, 61, 85–86
Bryant, David J., 86–87
"Buffered self," 108, 110
Burgess, John P., 134–35

Calvin, John, 107, 128, 136
Calvinists, 107
Campbell, Ted A., 117–18
Canonical test, 91, 94–95
Christological test, 91, 94–95
Chronic anxiety, 110–13
Communities of faithful practice, 134–37
Cross-cultural mission, 139
Crossing boundaries, 137–40

Deism, 108–10
Development terms, 16–17
Diversity, 116–17
Dream stories, 27, 33

Einstein, Albert, 81
El-roi, interpretation of, 58
"Examine" or "test," 65–67
Exclusive humanism, 108–10

Fractured body, 113–16
Friedman, Edwin, 111–12, 130–31, 132–33

General Assembly, 141
Gifted members, 116–18
"God of seeing," 58

149

Index

"God who sees," 58, 60
God's hospitality, 61–62
God's self-disclosure, 92–95

Hagar, 56–60
Heart, Hebrew concept of, 37–38
Heifetz, Ronald A., 118–20

Imagination, 81–89, 103, 105–6
   category in theology, 83–87
   multidisciplinary approach
     required, 81–83
   multiple forms of, 83
   ordination questions exemplify
     place of, 87–88
Intention in strategic management, 7

Jinkins, Michael, 106
Judgment, 40–41, 48, 95

Kotter, John P., 5, 38–39

Leadership, 129–34
   characteristics needed, 131–34
   rationale for attention to, 130
Long term and adaptive challenges, 121–22, 123

Maitland, Sara, 88–89
Man born blind, 95–101
Management technique(s), 8–9
Mancini, Will, 10, 13–15, 18, 20, 39–40, 44
Mediator, 12
Medieval assumptions, 107
Mission futures, 139–40

Nanus, Burt, 4, 38
Neuroscience, 80–81, 101

Pentecost, 63–64
Philosophical and religious
   context, 106–10

Philosophical foundations of
   organizations, 20–21
Political polarization, 115–16
Postexilic vision stories, 33
Precondition for peace, 61
Priesthood of all believers, 11–12
Protestant Reformation, 107, 110
Proverbs 29:18, 70–73
   context, 70–71
   poetic structure, 71
   translation, 73
   vocabulary, 71–73

Rad, Gerhard von, 46–47
"Religious vision," 92
Resources, 17
Rodgers, Daniel T., 114–15
Russian Orthodoxy
   challenge to Protestantism, 135–36
   view of humankind's purpose, 135

Secular age, 106–10
Secularity, types of, 106–7
Seeing
   brain activity in mental seeing, 80
   fallible and sinful, 79, 90
   and feelings, 92
   forms of, 74–75, 96
   and God's creation, 77–78, 90
   and God's special revelation, 92–95
   and God's use or
     transformation of, 90–91
   mental, 80–81, 89–91, 101–2
   physical, 75–79, 101–3
   physiology of eyesight, 75–76
   revelatory, 91–95, 101–3
   sign of God's love, 78–79, 90
Senge, Peter, 1–4, 38
Short term and technically
   focused, 118–22, 123

Index

Sin, 12
Small, Joseph D., 128–29
Spirit-vision relationship, 63–64
Spirit's gifts, 63–64
Spirit's outpouring, 63
"Spiritual vision," 92
Stacy, Ralph, 6–7, 39, 42
Structural alignment, 14–15
Swan, Sandra, 15–18, 20, 39–40, 44

Tax collector, 67–68
Taylor, Charles, 106–10
Technical leadership, 119–20
Technical work, 118, 120–21
Theological conversation, 123–29
 in Geneva's Venerable
  Company, 128
 opportunities for, 127–28
 rationale for, 124–27
Theological foundations of church
 organizations, 20–21
Theophany, 31–32
Transmission of the faith, 137–38

Vision
 benefits of, 3–5, 12–14, 18
 Bible's understanding of, 21
 in church organizations, 10–21
 comparisons between secular
  and church organizations,
  18–19
 definitions of, 3–6, 11, 13,
  17–18, 74–75
 as disclosure, 91–95, 101–3
 as energizing force, 1–2, 4–6, 8
 and feelings, 92
 and God's special revelation,
  92–95
 God's use or transformation of,
  90–91
 implications for trust in God,
  54–55
 impossible, 6–7, 103
 individual vs. communal
  implications, 53–54
 mental, 80–81, 83, 89–91,
  101–3
 and organizational servitude,
  2–3, 5, 8, 12, 15
 as pointer and preparation,
  46–53
 purpose(s) of, 46–53, 102
 recipients of, 6, 11, 13, 44–46,
  102
 in secular organizations, 1–9
 sensory, 75–79, 101–2
 source(s) or origin of, 3–4, 6,
  9, 11, 13, 18, 35–39, 91–92,
  102–4
 subjects, 39–41, 69, 102
 tamed, 2–6
 time perspectives in, 19, 42–44,
  77, 90, 102
 triumphal, 103–4
 types of, 74–75, 101–2
Vision Team, 141–43
Visioning processes, 3–6, 8, 12–14
 assumptions in, 6–9, 15
 in church practice, 101–4
 questionable rationale for, 69
"Visual imagination," 83
Vocabulary of seeing, 23–28, 23n1,
 35, 58, 60, 95–96

Walls, Andrew, 137–39
Warnock, Mary, 81–83
Wilder, Amos, 83–85

Yoder, Christine Roy, 70–71

www.ingramcontent.com/pod-product-compliance
Lightning Source LLC
Chambersburg PA
CBHW071505150426
43191CB00009B/1419